Disney Unbuilt

A Pocket Guide to the
Disney Imagineering Graveyard

Chris Ware

Theme Park Press
www.ThemeParkPress.com

Theme Park Press publishes its books in a variety of print and electronic formats. Some content that appears in one format may not appear in another.

Editor: Bob McLain
Layout: Artisanal Text

ISBN 978-1-68390-032-0
Printed in the United States of America

Theme Park Press | www.ThemeParkPress.com
Address queries to bob@themeparkpress.com

Contents

Introduction

Disney has made many dreams a reality. While we all are familiar with what Disney *did* make, many of us are not familiar with are the projects that never made it off the drawing board. Together we will look at all the parks, lands, attractions, and restaurants never built.

We will see what could have been. We will learn why these dreams never became real. We will also see that with Disney a good dream never dies, but often gets incorporated into other something else.

You are sure to find some great ideas you wish Disney had built and some others that you're glad they never did.

Parks

Of all the Disney dreams that never make it beyond the land of imagination, entire parks are the saddest. Parks feature entire lands and many rides that will never see a single guest enjoy them. While you may not love the general idea or theme of a park, there is bound to be at least a ride or attraction that you will wish that Disney would have made.

The development of a whole park may show the company's commitment to the project, but because of the expense it can also be harder to see the final concept realized.

Reality all too often ruins great ideas. Even for the parks that do get built, they often do not achieve the size and scope of their original plans. Often things have to be cut back to meet budgets and deadlines.

The parks in this section share one thing in common: they would not be built. But some elements of them may have ended up in other parks later, as Disney is a fan of recycling.

Mickey Mouse Park

Mickey Mouse Park would have been the very first Disney park built. It ultimately would lead to the creation of Disneyland. The park would have been across the street from the Disney Studio on an 8-acre lot. Walt had wanted to let the public see how animation was made and let them see the studio, but he felt there was not much to really see. To add to the studio experience he felt that a park would be a good fit.

Disney hired Harper Goff who was working for Warner Brothers at the time to work on the initial concept art for the park. Harper Goff would end up being one of Disney's Imagineers and work on many other Disney projects.

The plans for Mickey Mouse Park were very similar to Disneyland. It would feature a Main Street similar to the one we know now. Of course a train would surround the park just like in the Disneyland parks around the world. There would be a stern-wheeler that would take you around an island just like in Disneyland. Walt even wanted pack mules just like he would have at Disneyland.

It didn't take long before Walt realized this small plot of land would not be able to hold all of his ideas. The reason Mickey Mouse Park was never made was because it became something bigger. Ultimately, it would become Disneyland. The story of Mickey Mouse Park may be the happiest ending for a Disney project that never got built.

Walt Disney's Riverfront Square

Walt Disney's Riverfront Square could have been the second Disney park. The park was in planning and developement from 1963-65. It was to be in St. Louis, Missouri. St. Louis was preparing for its bicentennial celebration and was working on major renovations and development of the the riverfront area.

One unique feature of the park is that it would be indoors. This would allow for year-round attendance.

The park was planned to be housed in a building five stories tall. The plan was to have artificial lighting to simulate the weather and time.

Main Street was to be based on St. Louis and New Orleans. The top floor of the building would have overlooked the Mississippi and featured a bar, lounge, banquet hall, and restaurant. Many concession stands and stores were included in the plans.

The park would have received many popular rides. Pirates of the Carribean, the Haunted Mansion, and a western river boat ride were to be included. A Lewis & Clark Adventure ride was planned. This ride would not make it to St. Louis, but it would come up again a few more times as we will see later and ultimately lead to a ride that would be built. Rides would be built for Mike Fink as well as Davy Crockett. Another attraction would be based on the Meramec Caverns. The park would include two Circarama theatres with one featuring a show about St. Louis. Plans were made for dark rides including Peter Pan, Snow White, and Pinocchio. This would have been the first time Pinocchio got its own ride in the park. Ultimately, Pinocchio would make it into other parks. Some of the minor attractions would include a wishing well, aviary, and explorable pirate ship.

There are conflicting stories as to why the park was never built. The most often cited story is that August Busch of the Busch brewing company said that a park that did not serve alcohol would never work in the state. This seems unlikely to be the real reason as Walt was going to allow alcohol in one location of the park. The real reason appears to be a variety of issues which include disagreements over ownership and financing.

While the park would never be built, it would see many of its ideas ultimately find their way into other projects and ultimately into the parks. Some of Disney's most famous rides such as Pirates of the Caribbean would end up being made shortly. Others would take some time such as Pinocchio, and Lewis & Clark would inspire Grizzly River Run.

Disneyland New York

Disneyland New York was to be placed where the New York World's Fair had been. Walt Disney had wanted to build a second park on the East Coast. He already had some attractions that were popular in place and figured it would be easy to convert the rest of the area to a theme park. New York having such a high population made sense to Disney.

However, another location was believed to be a possible alternative. That location was Florida. After much research, Florida was presented to Walt as the better alternative. One main reason was the better weather that would allow for year-round operations while New York could expect much lower attendance in the winter months. Another factor was the belief that people went to New York to see Broadway shows and tourist sites. People did not go to New York to visit theme parks.

Ultimately, Disneyland New York would not get made, but many of the existing rides that were already built and planned for the park would find homes in other Disney parks.

Port Disney

Port Disney was more then just a few drawings on paper. Port Disney was expected to be built. The story starts before Disneyland even opened. Walt Disney felt he needed to have a hotel nearby, but he barely had enough money to build Disneyland. For a while, Disney tried to convince a friend of his John "Jack" Wrather, a local businessman, to build the hotel. Wrather had no interest in building the hotel. Finally Walt gave a passionate speech to Wrather and by the end was in tears. After that Wrather relented and agreed to build the hotel.

You are probably wondering what a hotel has to do with an entire park. If you have not already figured it out, the hotel was the Disneyland Hotel. Not only did Wrather own the hotel right next door to Disneyland, he also owned the right to the Disney name for other hotels in the area. Owning the hotel right next to the park and the naming rights was a thorn in the side of Disney for some time. For a long while Disney tried to get Wrather to sale the hotel and the naming rights. Wrather never would.

What made it possible for Disney to finally get the rights was the death of Wrather in 1984. His company got into financial trouble and was ripe for a hostile takeover at a time when hostile takeovers were all the rage on Wall Street. Disney went in with a foreign company to buy Wrather's company. At first they were unwilling. But once Disney mentioned the lease on the monorail to the hotel would soon expire and they may have to change the daily cost for its use they relented. Disney later bought out the other company and gained full control of Wrather's company.

Wrather had a company with many parts that were not all connected. Disney sold most of them off. They did keep some things they thought might be useful, such as rights to some TV and film properties like the Lone Ranger. The Disneyland Hotel and local naming rights were the main reason for the purchase. With the purchase came some extras that Disney thought they could use.

Disney ended up the owner of the *Spruce Goose*, *Queen Mary*, and land in Long beach. It was this part of the Wrather empire that Disney decided would be a good fit for a new park. The Long Beach property was to include a marina, cruise ship port, retail and entertainment district, hotels, and of course a theme park, DisneySea.

The park would be both entertaining and educational. It would be an aquatic version of Epcot or a giant version of the Living Seas. There would be actual research as well as educational programs geared toward youth and schools. DisneySea would have included a shark encounter in a shark cage. A Mysterious Island land was to have a simulator ride called Nemo's Lava Cruiser. Pirate Island was also planned. Other planned lands included Hero Harbor and Fleets of Fantasy. The Port Disney resort itself would also include a monorail that went around the resort and a shuttle service for the 20+ miles to Disneyland.

The park went far into development. Schematics for some attractions were made. Models were built. Disney went so far as to create a publication for the local residents called *The Port Disney News*. This publication is where most of the information about the planned area comes from.

Many factors would conspire against the park. The first, and one we will see many times for projects during this decade, is that money was being tied up in Disneyland Paris. The company had multiple projects in the works and only one might ultimately make it. While local city officials were in favor of the development it came up against opposition from the California Coastal Commission. The plan required Disney to dredge up part of the ocean to create more land. Disney offered to settle on a smaller amount of land, but they still could not get the go ahead. Disney went so far so to try to pass a bill that would give them an exemption and allow them to create the land. The bill did not pass. There were also other concerns by local authorities about bringing to many people into an already busy port environment.

At this point the park was pretty much dead in the water. But the final nail in the coffin was that Anaheim offered Disney a real sweetheart deal. They would give Disney its own on ramp, reroute power and other necessities, and even help with the financing of a parking structure. That meant if a third park was to be built it would be built in Anaheim.

While the Port Disney project never made it you probably already know what happened to the DisneySea park. The park with its name intact would go on to become Tokyo DisneySea. While it would not be the exact same, many aspects would remain. Lands such as the Mysterious Island would remain but with ride changes. Even some of the hotel ideas would merge into the DisneySea Hotel MiraCosta. Besides getting an entire park with the same name built overseas, the Pirate Island may have been inspiration for the Pirate land in Shanghai Disneyland.

While it may be a long time, it still may be possible that some form of DisneySea will be built. After all, talk of a third gate has been around for a while. It is possible that when a third gate was announced by Michael Eisner it was going to be a DisneySea park. With so many projects including major renovations at Disneyland, however, it is unlikely the third gate will open any time soon. It may even end up as a fifth gate in Disney World. Even if Disney never builds another DisneySea, some of it rides and attractions could pop up elsewhere.

Disney-MGM Studio Backlot

You may be thinking Disney made an MGM studios park; they just renamed it later. You are right, but the Disney MGM Studio Backlot was going to be located in Burbank, not Orlando. The history of the park begins even before the Orlando park opened. Disney got wind of Universal's plans to build a park in Orlando. The park would be designed with former Imagineers and be similar to a Disney park in that it would feature rides more than a tram that took you to the attractions.

Disney had already had some similar plans in the works on a smaller scale for Epcot as we will see later. However, with Orlando trying to get a toehold on the Disney's Orlando kingdom, Disney went ahead and announced its plans to build a similar park in hopes of stopping Universal.

However, Universal would not be swayed. Disney then decided to go after Universal on its home turf in California. Disney got a great deal with the city of Burbank to build what at first would be a mall but over time would turn into more of a full-fledged theme park mall hybrid.

The plans included a simulator ride and a board-walk-themed area which would include a Ferris wheel that went below the lake. The main attraction would have been a copy of the Great Movie Ride that made it into the Orlando park. There would be an Old West town. The park would also house animation, TV, and movie production areas where guests could get a behind-the-scenes glimpse of how Disney productions are made.

There would also be lots of shopping and dining much like a normal mall. There would be an ice and roller skating rink. A movie theatre complex would also be present. There would be a 6-story parking structure. An area similar to Pleasure Island even with some of the same names for the venues would be included as well. There would be a large hotel themed to the hey day of Hollywood. One fun idea was to have a boat poised to go over the edge of cliff as a restaurant.

Disney had support from the city of Burbank. But Universal was a mean adversary. Not only did Universal sue Disney, they also sent out pamphlets to local residents to turn them against the project. MGM also was giving Disney a tough time saying the agreement was only good for Orlando, not Burbank.

Disney's partner in the project was a company we will hear more about later, Jim Rouse Enterprise Development Company, which was in charge of the retail aspect of the park. They could not find enough retail outlets interested in the project. Most likely the cost of the project would be much higher than a typical mall and the higher price tag was not believed to be worth the cost to the retail outlets who turned down the company.

The other main reason it never got built was the original price tag for the park had doubled. While it was still believed it would be profitable, it was not going to be as profitable. Also, Disney had other projects in the works that were given priority. The first was Disney-MGM Studios and the second EuroDisneyland.

While the park never got built, aspects of it did get built. Downtown Disney would be similar but smaller in size to the planned Burbank project. A larger parking structure would get built in Anaheim as well. The Pier area would end up in California Adventure including the Ferris Wheel that went below the water line.

Disney's America

Disney's America was planned for Haymarket, Virginia. The park would have focused on the history of America as told the way only Disney could. It was a pet project of Michael Eisner who is a fan of history and felt that with Disney's strong ability to tell an engaging story it could offer a wonderful way to introduce young people to the history of this great nation.

The project started with a trip to Colonial Williamsburg and it was decided that Disney could do something similar but better. Then Disney went on to option about 2300 acres of land from Exxon. This gave them the ability to buy the land if they decided to, but they did not have to. They did not let Exxon know that they were going to buy the land because they were afraid if they knew they would want more money for it. Disney also had some other land they were looking at which would make a total of 3000 acres.

The land was about 20 minutes from Washington, D.C., and near many historic locations including the site of the Battle of Manassas took place. Not only would Disney's America be about American history it would be right in the middle of historic U.S. locations. At the time it seemed like a perfect fit.

Disney's America would feature 9 themed lands. The first land that you would enter by crossing under a train trestle would be Crossroads USA. This would be the park's version of Main Street but based in the Civil War era. There would be a Civil War encampment and costumed Union as well as Rebel soldiers. As with many other parks, steam trains would be located here that would take guests around the park.

A Native America land would have a Powhatan village in keeping with Disney's *Pocahantas* property. Other local tribes would also be represented. In the land guests would experience interactive experiences and arts and crafts. The main attraction would have been a Lewis and Clark Expedition which would have been a white water rafting ride. So yet again the Lewis and Clark Expedition from Walt Disney's Riverfront Square had a shot at getting made. Concept art also shows a canoe ride as a possible attraction in this section of the park.

Next, guests would encounter the Civil War Fort. Guests could see a re-enactment of the battle between the *Monitor* and *Merrimac*. Battle re-enactments would also take place in this area. The fort itself would house a 360-degree film about the Civil War. Some discussion was even made about a slave experience which would utilize virtual reality.

We the People would be a re-creation of Ellis Island. There would be restaurants here along with live shows. The main feature of the area would be a musical

Muppet show about immigration. While it may not sound particularly exciting, it is an area that Michael Eisner was particularly fond of.

The next area would have been known as State Fair. This area would have had a show about baseball. Little information is known about the show and if it would use actors or audio animatronics, for instance. Some concept art shows a baseball diamond outside so it may be where the show was to take place. A Ferris wheel would also be in this section of the park. The most exciting ride of this land would be a wooden roller coaster. There may have been some other carnival-style rides included as well in this area. The food would have been standard fair food such as hot dogs.

The next section would be the Family Farm. The time period would be during the Depression and the Dust Bowl. Guests would be able to experience a wedding, barn dance, and a buffet. Guests would get the chance to milk real cows and make their own ice cream. Yes, they planned to make you work on your vacation.

Presidents Square would focus on the birth of American democracy. The main attraction for Presidents Square would be an updated version of the Hall of Presidents which would be housed in a replica of Independnce Hall.

Enterprise would have been a factory town. American ingenuity and work ethic would have been the theme here. Former technology of the era as well as future technologies would be showcased somewhat like Innoventions or the Carousel of Progress. The big attraction would have been a roller coaster known as the Industrial Revolution. The coaster would have taken riders through a factory and have them come close to the simulated fire of a blast furnace.

Victory Field would be the final land of the park. It would be a World War II airfield. Planes from various times would be on display. There would be virtual reality-based attractions focusing on military flight. The first version of Soarin' was conceived for this land. Finally, a dueling coaster was envisioned. Due to the cost of the coaster it was scrapped early on. The coaster would have had a U.S. and a German track. At one point you would nearly miss a tank. Many times during the ride you would nearly miss the other coaster.

Michael Eisner really wanted to have a hotel in a park and it was planned that this park would finally be the one that did this. There were even plans for an RV park. A golf course was planned as well. There also would be a retail and commercial district. They even had plans to build homes and an entire community with schools and a library.

At first the project started out well with support from both the outgoing and the incoming state governors who saw it could bring revenue to the state. Some historians had also been positive about the idea. However, Disney had to keep things secret at first for the land deal with Exxon to go through without having to pay more. So they were not able to reach out to as many people and groups in advance to get a general idea of any problems or concerns about the park.

The park got very close to being made. Lots of concept art was drawn. Models were built. They even made an official announcement that they were building it.

When Disney finally announced plans for Disney's America, it quickly faced a great deal of backlash.

Many concerns were brought up. Some felt it inappropriate to build a theme park so near to bona-fide historical locations. Some felt people would skip the real historical locations for the Disney version. Many people did not like the name as they felt it was Disney saying they owned America.

Another major problem was it was located near a very influential part of the state. The area is home to some of the most powerful families in the country. They were not happy with the idea and had the power to use the media as well as politicians to stop the project.

The biggest reason for the failure of the park was the local opposition. However, many more problems would rise up to make sure Disney's America never arrived in Haymarket. At the time Frank Wells died which was a major blow to the studio as he was the second in command. Jeffrey Katzenberg wanted Well's job, but Michael Eisner would not give it to him right away so he left the company. Eisner had to undergo triple bypass surgery. It was not a banner year for the company. On top of that they were still reeling from the Euro Disneyland fiasco. Although at just over $600 million, Disney's America would have been the cheapest of all the new parks being looked at, and so relatively affordable.

However, to top off all of that, they went back to the original projections which showed a profit from the start and found that would not be the case. They had expected a year round park but ultimately decided it would have to be closed for 3-4 months of the year. The lower-than-expected Euro Disney numbers also made then re-evaluate their estimates on total visitors. After these new factors were factored in, it was shown that the park would not operate profitably as expected.

While this may seem like the end of the Disney's America, it still had one more chance. The park would not end up in Haymarket, Virginia, but that did not mean it would not be made at all. Disney had been planning to make a second park for Disneyland for some time. Perhaps a way could be found to bring Disney's America to Disneyland as the second park there.

Instead of building from scratch, it might be possible to take work off of an already existing park. Not far from Disney lay Knotts Berry Farm, the park that the other Walt built. Walt Disney and Walter Knott were actually friends. Around the time the Disney's America plan fell through and Disney was still looking into what to do for a second park, the Knott family began looking for someone to buy their park in nearby Buena Park.

Disney looked at it and at first were not impressed until they saw a separate area that had a reproduction of Liberty Hall. The plan was to improve this area of land to add more buildings and to ultimately add a Hall of Presidents show. This would be the new entrance to the park.

Other areas would require some tweaking but could be turned into areas that would fit with the theme. Bigfoot Rapids would loose the Big Foot and gain Lewis and Clark. Mystery Lodge would remain and tie the area in with a Native American theme. It looked like the Lewis and Clark ride would finally get built. The Ghost Town would also be part of this area but with an emphasis on Western Expanison.

The Roaring 20's section of the park would become the Enterprise territory which would eventually get the Industrial Revolution roller coaster. Reflection Lake was going to be turned into Freedom Bay which would get an Ellis Island building.

One advantage of the proposed park would be that they could keep it open the entire time and be making money from the start. Changes could be done in phases. While one phase was being worked on the rest of the park would be able to operate.

While this may sound like a great plan it had some problems. The park was almost 8 miles from Disneyland. A monorail line was quickly deemed too expensive as well as impractical. A bus system was also discussed but concerns were made over liability issues, although as you already saw with Port Disney, it would not be as far to go. Michael Eisner was not particularly fond of the idea, believing that Disney should build its own parks and if it just replaced something it would take away from what made Disney special in the first place. The biggest problem was that the Knott family rejected the plan fearing that the park their family had built would be changed completely by Disney. The family instead sold the park to Cedar Fair, the company that owns the Cedar Point amusement park. Cedar Fair would go on to make more changes and remove more of the original Knott's Berry Farm than Disney had planned to do.

You may have already guessed some of what would become of Disney's America. Many aspects of the park would go into Disney California Adventure. The State Fair area became Paradise Pier with the roller coaster becoming California Screamin' and the Ferris wheel also being brought into the park. The Lewis and Clark Expedition which had been trying to get made since Walt Disney's Riverfront Square would finally get built in some form as the Grizzly River Rapids. Condor Flats would be inspired by Victory Field. Soarin' Over California would be taken from Victory Field and turned into a modern ride over California but using the same idea and planned technology. The Family Farm would be brought back in a small way as Bountiful Valley Farm.

WestCOT

Just from the name you can probably get a pretty good idea what WestCOT would be like. If you thought it would be a West Coast version of Epcot, then you would be right. Being a newer park, though, it would be an update of the East Coast version, though smaller. After all, you can fit Disneyland inside the Seven Seas Lagoon so they have a bit more space to work with in Florida.

Just like Epcot, WestCOT would be divided into two areas. One area would be a world showcase-like area. Because of size restraints each country would not get its own pavilion but pavilions would be based on regions. Also to give more space many of the structure would build up, giving more space to work with on the same parcel of land. Besides giving more floor space, this also would allow for more control of things like lighting. The plan was that this would also allow for easier changes to set pieces. If a new development came, a new building would not be built but new facades would be built. Also the inside would not be exposed to the elements so they would last longer with only the outside of the buildings needing the more intensive maintenance that outside locations require.

Imagineers also felt that the environment would get guests immersed. At Epcot the pavilions are small and you can see the lagoon all the time as a constant reminder of where you really are. With a show building all you see and experience is the show with nothing outside to distract guests even if it is a nice view of Eiffel Tower or other scenic pavilion structure.

The first location you would enter at WestCOT would be an American Pavilion. The American Pavilion would be much like the Epcot version but with an updated and improved show. Next to America would be America's neighbors, Mexico and Canada. Mexico would be the Central American area and feature a show similar to the Mystery Lodge at Knott's Berry Farm based on the Aztec and Inca, a dark ride, a restaurant, and thrill rides. It was said it would be a more lively version of the Epcot Mexico Pavilion. On the other side of America would be Canada that would also have a show even more closely resembling the Mystery Lodge as it would be based on Native American culture.

The next area would be Europe. Europe would feature a Tivoli Garden-inspired area with attractions to entertain. A lesson the Imagineers learned from Epcot was many of the pavilions were just shops and restaurants with a few shows and that the younger audience found it boring. So they wanted to incorporate things to do for all ages in each location. Europe would also have a 360-degree film with audio animatronics that had been made for Paris originally named "From Time to Time." This would become known in the Magic Kingdom as the Timekeeper. The show would be located under the Acropolis. The E-ticket attraction of the land would be the Trans-European Express which was to be an exciting chase on European railroads as you go by famous European landmarks.

The Asia land would have a steel coaster known as Ride the Dragon. The ride would have traditional Chinese dragons at the front. The coaster would have guests go on mountains known as the Dragons Teeth. At the very top of the roller coaster you would be able to see out of the park so Disney planned to put streaming silks around the area so you would not see outside of the world they had created. Asia would have a Japanese show, possibly the Meet the World show that had been planned for Epcot but got sent to Tokyo. The Temple of Heaven from the China Pavilion at Epcot would also be used again which may have also included the movie that Epcot has as well. There would also be a South East Asia section. A carousel of mythical Asian animals would be in Asia, along with an Indian-themed hotel.

The African and Middle East section had a couple of concepts that Imagineers were excited about but got cut before anything else. The plan was to have a Great Religions of the World show which got axed because of concerns of offending anyone. A similar idea was to have a Seven Days of Creation show and have seven world-renowned artists each work on a single day. That was not outright canceled but put on the back burner for a possible later phase.

The African area would feature a river raft ride down the fictional Congobezi River. This may have been part of the inspiration for both Kali River Rapids as well as Grizzly River Run which ended up in roughly the same area. Under a large African tree African folk tales would be told. The Tishman African Art

Exhibit was to find a permanent home at the Africa Pavilion. Other outdoor entertainment such as drummers would be present. Demonstrations of traditional farming methods would be shown. A second-phase Egyptian building was also already being planned. The Egyptian building would be a hotel and possibly offer more attractions as well.

Connecting all the areas together would be the longest boat ride in Disney history. The full boat ride which was to be known as the River of Time would take a full 45 minutes to complete. But like the Train in Disneyland you would have the chance to get on and off at various locations. Each stop would allow you to get off if you wanted. You could then board the ride where you got off and continue the boat ride. The ride itself would have given you a tour of the history and culture of the places you would go to.

The Future World Pavilion would all be housed in one building. Initial designs called for a geodesic sphere like in Epcot but on a much grander scale and to be painted gold. The original plans were for the sphere to be 300 feet compared to Epcot's 180 feet tall sphere. The sphere was never going to make it. The size of the sphere would have made it the largest building in Orange County. The sphere received large opposition from local home owners who viewed it as an eyesore as well as creating too much light pollution. The sphere had no chance of making it into the park as smaller versions continued to face opposition. Disney worked on figuring out a wienie for the park but never came up with a satisfactory focal point.

The Future World Pavilion would feature many of the pavilions that were located in Epcot but often with upgrades. A Nature section would combine the Seas and the Land. It too would have growing areas as well as new additions not seen in Florida. You would get to experience multiple environments including desert, jungle, and even arctic which would include snow that you could play with. The Seas area would have been very similar to the Epcot version. One major difference was while both pavilions in Epcot offer behind-the-scenes tours, WestCOT was to make these a regular part of the experience instead of limited up charge activities.

Living would combine the Wonders of Life Pavilion with the Imagination Pavilion. The Wonders of Life section would include Body Wars, Cranium Command, and the Making of Me. The Imagination Pavilion would feature a similar but unique version of the Journey into Imagination ride. It sounds like some of the changes would be to take some of the unused ideas that were originally planned for the Epcot version and finally build them in the WestCOT version.

A Science section would be new but may have been where rides which were planned for the park such as Horizons, Universe of Energy, and World of Motion would be placed. The section would have some unique things of its own. The first would be a hands-on interactive area for kids. The idea behind the area was that Disney found kids do not know much about modern jobs. Someone who goes to work on a computer everyday is not the same as someone that does something like farm, so the exhibits would help give kids an idea about jobs. The most exciting part would be a new ride which was to be known as Cosmic Journeys. The ride would be similar to Adventures of Inner Space in that you would shrink but it would also make you expand as well. The ride was to be a combination of film, simulation, and 3D which sounds a lot like a 3D simulator like the new version of Star Tours.

On top of all this there is some speculation that a Space Pavilion was also planned. It is possible that Space may have included Horizons as Horizons was said to be part of the park but no particular area was given for the location. The Space Pavilion planned for Epcot may be what has made some think it was also planned for WestCOT. Since little evidence exists that it would have been included, we will save the discussion about the Space Pavilion for the Epcot lands that were never built.

On top of all this there would also be a monorail. Where the monorail would go is unclear. Besides the monorail a PeopleMover system above ground would take guests from the parking lot to the two Disneyland Resort park entrances.

With the idea of the park having most pavilions indoors, the plan was to have the first few floors dedicated to the theme park. The upper levels would house the hotel areas for guests. They would have been the first hotels inside of a Disney park. This idea would carry over to DisneySea as well as California Adventure.

The project went very far. Announcements were made in various media. Plenty of concept art was made for all the different areas and attractions. Models were even built. So the project came close to becoming a reality.

The entire plan would have cost $3.1 billion. On top of that it is common in the theme park industry to have cost overruns so it is likely that the cost would have been much higher. Obviously the project was going to be very expensive. The project was also part of an even more extensive plan to expand the Disneyland Resort and more of those plans will be covered later.

To make such massive expansions, Disney had to have the support of the city and even higher government authorities. Disney even wanted to be given complete and full power with a special district to be created such as with Disney World and the Reedy Creek Improvement District. Disney never was able to make such an arrangement. From the very start the project was plagued with problems. Some of the problems included opposition from locals, an example of this being previously mentioned as the complaints for the park's giant sphere.

Not only would major changes and improvements be needed in the immediate vicinity but outside changes would be needed for things such as the freeway. All that Disney needed and wanted it couldn't get. It did what it could and was able to eventually get some things from local authorities but not nearly as much as it had hoped.

As with so many projects during this time, WestCOT was partially derailed because of the financial problems caused by Disneyland Paris. Michael Eisner planned a retreat with Imagineers and other Disney leaders in Aspen. He had decided WestCOT would not work so he wanted to come up with another alternative. It was at this meeting the the idea for Disney California Adventure would come up.

It may seem that Disney California Adventure was a better deal at only $600 million, but they spent another $100 million before current CEO Bob Iger would ultimately put in $1.1 billion into the expansion. So Disney California Adventures ended up costing $1.8 billion, not as much as the WestCOT plan but most people would probably agree that WestCOT would have been a better park. Also, it would have been completed at one time and it is likely that unlike California Adventure which struggled the first few years to gain an audience WestCOT may have seen much greater attendance right from the start. Even if they had scaled the project back, a scaled down version of the park would probably have been better received then California Adventure was initially.

With regular rumors of a third Disneyland Resort park it is possible that some of these ideas will see the light of day once more. It is possible that instead of building a totally new park they will take what they have and create a WestCOT after all.

Lava Lagoon

Lava Lagoon was to be an indoor water park at Disneyland Paris. The park was to have a tropical theme and be housed under a glass dome. Even though it is hard to find information, it appears that the park was far along as it went beyond the drawing board to having models made.

It appears there would have been a volcano in the middle of the park which would have been named the Big Kahuna. Some other rides or areas of the park would be Aloha Falls and Kahuka Falls. Around the park would be a lazy river. The park would have many tropical plants and tropical elements such as Tiki statuary. The volcano would feature many slides with the idea that they naturally formed from cooled lava flows. The park would also feature a wave pool.

The park would not all be located indoors; there would also be a seasonal outdoor area. Most of the outside venues would be restaurants, saunas, and shops. However, there would be a couple of water rides open outside.

Like many projects planned during this period, financial problems caused by Disneyland Paris would keep the park from ever getting built. However, rumors have swirled for years that Paris may get a third gate. It is often speculated when these rumors come up that Lava Lagoon may rise after all.

Disney is legally required to build something in 2017 which most understand that to be an actual park, though some question the wording and believe anything could be built by Disney to fulfill their legal obligations. With the failure of Walt Disney Studios Park, if the legal team at Disney do not think they can get by building anything, a water park could be a cheaper alternative with less risk.

Dark Kingdom

Dark Kingdom would have been a theme park devoted to the villains. The original idea for an entire park came about with a concept for a villain-based ride for the Magic Kingdom which we will discuss in more detail later.

The wienie of the park would be Maleficent's castle. The park would have an area for Scar, the Wicked Queen, and Captain Hook. Rides that were considered include an Ursula ride similar to Dumbo. A Night on Bald Mountain roller coaster was a possibility. Dark rides would have included a Cruella De Ville ride and a Captain Hook ride. It was rumored that the emphasis would be on thrill rides to better compete with Universal.

No reason is known why this park never got created. It is most likely that other projects took precedence such as Animal Kingdom, and Disney just does not have enough money to build everything it comes up with.

Some of the ideas would come back such as an Ursula ride which would not make it into a park but would show that some of the ideas are still floating around at Imagineering.

DisneyQuest

You may be thinking that DisneyQuest was built. You are right, but the many other DisneyQuest locations were never built. Disney got very close to opening many other locations. Announcements were made in local newspapers. DisneyQuest locations were being built and then were canceled; it doesn't get any closer than that.

A short-lived DisneyQuest Chicago existed. It was the failure of this location that led to the end of work on the DisneyQuest Philadelphia location that was already underway. The locations were to be all about the same. Disney did have plans to add in new attractions at a location and then roll them out to others at various times. However, that never happened.

Besides a Philadelphia location that was under construction, an Anaheim location was planned for Downtown Disney. The Anaheim location never got past the drawing board.

One problem that killed the parks was the rapid speed of technological development. Moore's Law predicts computing power to double every 18 months. That means to stay current every two years you need new technology to stay on the cutting edge. Disney also failed to realize that no standalone arcade has made it since the 1983 arcade crash. Perhaps some other attractions such as a Buzz Lightyear or Star Wars-themed Laser Tag could have anchored the arcade. Maybe an indoor mini-golf course. That DisneyQuest has done as well as it did is amazing and a testament to the Disney name. For over a decade the Orlando location has been able to do what no other standalone arcade has been able to since the 80s.

Disneyland's Third Park

While it has been rumored for years a third park would be built in California there was actually once an official announcement of a planned third gate at the California resort. The announcement was made in the annual stock report. No information was given about the park other than that it was going to be built and a single piece of concept art was shown that didn't reveal much.

It is possible that it may have been a DisneySea-style park. As has been discussed earlier, this idea would not be new to the area. With a version finally being built overseas it may have provided a theme park that was well received, but with R&D already spent on some or most of the rides that may come to the U.S. it may have been a cheap option. A carbon copy of Tokyo would have been unlikely and in some cases such as Indiana Jones redundant. Even if the park would have taken a land or two and some popular rides it would have saved on some of the cost since R&D can be a large share of the expense.

This park was announced toward the end of the Eisner era. The park would have been built at the start of the Iger era. When Bob Iger took charge he decided that California Adventure needed to be fixed before a third park was built. So instead of a third park we got changes to California Adventure. While talk of a third park in California resurfaces regularly, Iger has gone so far as to state it is not happening any time soon. But that does not mean it will never happen.

Disney Wharf at Sydney Harbor

The Disney Wharf at Sydney Harbor didn't get much attention. The plan was rather grand. Not only would a theme park be built, but lots more. There would have been a marina, ferry wharf, light rail stations, themed hotels, retail space, office space, an upscale residential area, and an entertainment area.

What is known about the park make it sound as if it would be on the small side. Some rides such as Peter Pan, Dumbo, and Finding Nemo were to be included. Also, Bibbidi Bobbidi Boutique was mentioned. Being in its early stages, it is possible more would have been included as things developed.

Two factors killed the idea. The first was that it was received with mixed feelings by local authorities. Those that did have interest soon lost interest when they discovered all that Disney expected the local government to do to prepare the area's infrastructure. While the cost may have been high, the same location is currently an open unused lot. It may have been a large investment in the short term, it may have been worth the cost in the long term.

Disney's Arabia

Little is known about this attraction. It is often on lists of Disney attractions that were never built, but I have never seen any concept art or much information to prove it ever was an actual Disney idea.

Supposedly the park was to be opened in Dubai, but a list of planned Dubai projects do not include it. If it was ever really planned, the 2008 recession and a Dubai financial crisis ended its chance.

Night Kingdom

Night Kingdom may be one of the most unique of all park ideas. The entire concept of one of these ideas is unlike anything Disney has ever done. The park was to be open to a very limited number of people for a very limited time each day. It would start in a large version of the Explorers Club where you would have a similar experience as in the actual club, but cast members would be telling you what you would be about to experience. Multiple high-end restaurants would be included in the park cost. The park would give guests an adventure. There would be ziplines over crocodiles, treks to see animals with night vision, and close encounters with animals including interacting with hippos and penguins. There would also be a Broadway-style show.

The guest to cast member ratio would be 2 to 1. The price was to be in the $200-300 range. The park was to compete with SeaWorld which had a similar high-priced limited experience available. They had two possible hotels being planned depending on the popularity.

Later, a scaled-back version was announced as Disney's Jungle Trek. Ultimately, the idea got cut down considerably. In Animal Kingdom, Disney started the Wild Africa Trek. Some elements remained such as encounters with hippos, going on a bushwalk, and the zipline became a rope bridge but still over crocodiles.

There is also a rumor that this would be the name of a fifth park at Disney World based on villains. The villain-inspired theme park rumor has been going around for a while, so it is likely just someone got the names and stories mixed up.

Pirate Park

Most known concept art and theories are that the Pirate park would be a water park. It is possible that a whole Pirate park was being planned, or that there were plans for a water park as well. When the concept art first leaked rumors were that it was in the Blue Sky phase.

Some theories about the potential park are that Imagineers may have been told to work on some pirate-related work as the work came out during the height of the Pirates of the Caribbean movie craze. Perhaps no set plans were made and it simply was various ideas being thrown around relating to Pirates.

It is possible that some of these concepts helped lead to the Pirate area of Shanghai Disneyland. It is likely that more pirate work was made during this time and some of that could have been the inspiration for the Shanghai area.

Of course one of the biggest questions is where would such a park be located? Disneyland has been theorized as it would be a smaller way to fit a third park in a limited area. The limited area that Disney has to work with, though, may not allow for even a water park. While it is likely this never was likely to be built, it has been suggested previous to this concept art surfacing that a third park could be a water park.

Disney World is the other most likely location. River Country was one place that was theorized but there are safety problems with that location. It may be more likely that a whole new piece of land would be developed for such a park.

Finally there is an area of land near Hong Kong Disneyland also speculated to be a good fit.

While a pirate-themed water park may have been a big hit before, it may not have the same popularity it would have. Disney may have realized that making a full park to cash in on a franchise fad may not be the best idea. With another Pirate movie still to come out, it is possible this idea may get a second look. It has often been suggested that an easy way to get a third park for Disneyland would be to make a water park, so a Pirates park could fit the bill.

Disneyland Singapore

Disneyland Singapore is possibly the park with the least information known about it. Besides being located in Singapore, the only thing known is that it was supposedly going to be an indoor theme park.

Since so little information is known, it is hard to say why this never got built.

While it is possible Disneyland Singapore was nothing more then a rumor, the wealth of Singapore, its high population, and the fact that rival Universal has a park in Singapore makes it possible that Disney could build a park in Singapore someday.

Lands

Since lands are not as big as parks, they're less expensive and therefore more likely to actually make it off the drawing board. It is harder to keep many ideas together, though, and see everything work out to become a whole land. Sometimes a land may not make it, but a ride or attraction that was planned for a land may.

Disneyland

Even from the very beginning, Disneyland had plans for lands that would ultimately not make it into the park on opening day. Disneyland would set the trend for lands never being built. This trend would continue with Disneyland as well as other parks that would later be built. Here we will find lands that never made it into the original Disneyland.

Lilliputian Land

Lilliputian Land was one of the first lands planned for Disneyland that would never be built. It was first planned when the Disneyland park was being planned. Had things worked out for the Lilliputian Land, it would have opened with the park.

Lilliputian Land would have been north of Tomorrowland and east of Fantasyland. The land would have been a land of miniatures. It would have a boat ride as well as a small live steam engine like the one Walt had at his home.

A few problems came up. The first was the plan was to have small mechanical figures that would sing, dance, buy overpriced souvenirs, etc. Attempts were made to create these mechanical people, but they were too far ahead of their time. A problem that Disney's legal team was worried about was a child getting hurt from the live steam. So the train got axed.

While an entire land never made it, Disneyland did open with one ride straight from Lilliputian Land. The Canal Boats of the World became part of Fantasyland. Not long after, the ride would be changed to the Storybook Land Canal boats, greatly improving a ride which was not well received. The change also made it much more like the original Lilliputian Land except without a train or mechanical people. With Casey Jr it would still feature a little train; it would just be a bigger train. If only they would update the Storybook Land Canal boats to include miniature mechanical figures from the movies.

Treasure Island

Treasure Island was another part of the original plan that would not get made. The plan was for Treasure Island to be the home of the Mickey Mouse Club headquarters. The headquarters were to be in a hollow tree. What exactly a hollow tree has to do with the Mickey Mouse Club is beyond me.

While Treasure Island never was made at Disneyland, Tom Sawyer Island would eventually replace it. Besides being the initial idea that lead to Tom Sawyer Island, later Disney World would for a very short time have a Treasure Island which would not last long before being replaced with Discovery Island. The main connection was that they were named Treasure Island and that they were islands. No Mickey Mouse Club headquarters. They both did have the idea of an island play area to explore.

International Street

Eventually, Disneyland would plan to add some lands that were never part of the original park plans. At first, Imagineers would make suggestions to Walt on what to add to the park and hoped something got the go ahead. The first such project for a land would be International Street. International Street would be off Main Street like so many other similar projects we will soon see.

International Street would include restaurants as well as shops from various countries around the world such as Germany, Spain, Japan, France, and others. There would be live music in the center of the square.

A sign was put up saying that it would come in 1956 just one year after the park opened. Peep holes were placed which gave viewers a view of a 3D picture of the model for the street. Each year came and went so each year the sign had to change the date of the opening. By 1959 the signs changed to Liberty Street and International Street would be no more; or would it?

While International Street never was made, it would be inspirational to Epcot. In some ways you could say that it got a much better deal by becoming half of Epcot then just an off-shoot of Main Street.

Liberty Street

Liberty Street was to be next to the Opera House. It would have been a street from out of Colonial America. It would include a harbor, but that was about it. There would be a show which was to be named One Nation Under God. This show would have featured audio animatronics. It was originally slated to open in 1959 at the same time as Edison Square.

Though it made it as far as getting on some maps and being mentioned as a coming attraction, it would never really get built. While it would never be built the show would go onto become the Hall of Presidents and inspire Liberty Square at the Magic Kingdom. Even the American Pavilion at Epcot may have taken some inspiration from Liberty Square.

Edison Square

Edison Square was to be an offshoot of Main Street located where the Plaza Inn stands. The area would be a turn-of-the-century city that just got electricity. The center of town would have a statue of Thomas Edison. The main feature would be a show called Harnessing the Lightning that would focus on the history of electricity as well as how it changed our lives.

While the land was never built, it was announced. At one point it was to open Easter 1959. But Easter 1959 came and went with no Edison Square. Edison Square even showed up on park maps.

The show itself would become the Carousel of Progress. One possible reason this never was built was that at the time the audio animatronics were not as developed as they needed to be to pull off such a show. It would be five more years until the World's Fair would see the same show.

Chinatown

Chinatown may have been a bit more exciting as it would have been more exotic. It was also planned as a way to showcase some of the diversity of California. While the previous Main Street additions were possibly too ambitious, Chinatown would have a much simpler venture.

You can read more about the planned restaurant and show later on. Unlike the other Main Street additions this one may have gotten a bit closer to really opening. Disney was even able to get the Chung King company which was a canned Chinese food company to be willing to come on as a sponsor.

The restaurant would have a big impact on Disney even though it was never made. According to Harriet Burns, one of the Imagineers who worked on the project, the reason it was never made was Walt came back from a trip to San Francisco where he often liked to travel (this is one reason the Walt Disney Family Museum is located there). Having been to Chinatown in San Francisco he decided that California already had a real one and so did Los Angeles. So there was no need for one in Disneyland. However, at the same time he decided that he wanted to make a presidential audio-animatronic figure. Walt, having played Lincoln in a school play as a child, wanted to go with Lincoln. This would lead to the Lincoln show at the World's Fair.

Big City USA

Finally Disney started looking at locations outside of Main Street to build a new land. Big City USA was planned to be built where Toontown would end up going. Big City USA was part of a long-range master plan from the 1970s that discussed Disneyland's future for the next 25 years. The idea of planning so far ahead seems crazy now when plans are made and then cut based on if a franchise can be made off a movie. Even in the 70s, with so many publicly announced projects never making it, the idea that Disney could accurately predict what would happen that far is a bit of a stretch. Few of the actual plans made it, the Pinocchio ride and Thunder Mountain being exceptions.

While some of these plans had little information about them given in the master plan, Big City USA had a lot of information that gives us a better picture of this land. Big City USA was going to be on the opposite end of the park and the opposite in theme to Main Street. While Main Street would be a small town like Walt's boyhood home of Marceline, Big City USA would be New York of the same time.

Some of the odd additions would be food facilities including an automat which was a popular food option at the time similar to vending machines in our time but food was made on the premises. There would be other food venues as well such as a cafeteria and a deli which were also possible dining options.

Broadway shows are one thing that people visit New York for, and Big City USA was going to include similar caliber shows as well. One reason for the new land was to have a larger indoor show facility that could house more people then Disneyland currently had in places like the Golden Horseshoe Revue. One show that was under consideration was a Ziegfeld Follies-style dinner show. They planned to have at least one theater that would hold 3000 people which could help in getting people out of the hot sun on warm days as well as keep people out of the lines to help make those lines shorter.

Food and shows would not be the only things built in Big City USA. It was planned to have a Coney Island-style section with many popular rides that you would find at an old-style amusement park of the era. The rides that were under consideration were a Ferris wheel, paddle boats, and a roller coaster. These would not be the only rides in Big City USA. One final planned ride would take you on a time machine in a subway. It was to be an E-ticket attraction. Not much is known about this ride, however. Overall, the land was to help handle many more people in the park.

One of the main reasons this land never made it was it was planned at the same time that Disney was working on Epcot. Epcot was a priority for the company. Disney wanted to finish what Walt had started. Besides putting many people to work on the Epcot project, they also put a large amount of the company's financial resources into it as well. Had Epcot not been built at the time, it is possible that we would have a Big City USA instead of a Toontown.

While Big City USA is unlikely to ever get built, especially at Disneyland with its limited space, many ideas from Big City USA would go on to inspire other projects. The Coney Island-style rides and attractions would come up again and again in other projects until they would find their way to Paradise Pier. Even DisneySea would get a Ziegfeld theater in its American Waterfront section which was also partially based on Big City USA.

Mythica

Little is known about Mythica. What is known is that it was a planned land that would focus on Greek and Roman myths. There are some rides that will be discussed later that are sometimes attributed to Fantasyland that may have been meant for Mythica instead.

While Mythica the land never made it into the parks, the name ultimately did. DisneySea would see a Legend of Mythica show. It is possible that the name came from this proposed land.

Land of Legends

What is known about Land of Legends is that it is based on classic American folk tales such as Paul Bunyan. The area would be near Bear Country and was to be near the Discovery Bay area if Discover Bay had been built. It would have had the Western River Expedition which will be mentioned later as well as a Legends of Sleepy Hollow-based ride and a ride for The Saga of Windwagon Smith

This project never made it past the stuff of legend because Discovery Bay was never built.

The idea of American folk tales being featured would come up again but little came of it. A concept for the Haunted Mansion included a Legend of Sleepy Hollow section that never made it either. Some of these ideas keep getting tossed around, so perhaps some of them will come sailing into the real world.

World Holiday Land

World Holiday Land was an extension of the earlier Main Street lands that never were built. It was most heavily inspired by International Street. However, it was not planned to be built off of Main Street but beyond the Disneyland berm near New Orleans Square.

The world would be limited to just Europe. The areas to be included would be France, Germany,

Scandinavia, and the UK. There were plans to have a 360-degree film. There would be a dark ride featuring Scandinavian fairy tales. There were plans for a medieval England-themed ride. The German area was to include an simulated alpine skiing experience.

Epcot is one possible reason that World Holiday Land never got built. Another reason may have been there was just too much going on at the time.

While World Holiday Land never was built, some of the plans for it were. It is possible the film may have inspired a regular film for the France Pavilion. The Scandinavian dark ride would go on to become Maelstrom at the Norway Pavilion in Epcot. It is likely that the other ideas may have at least been suggested for Epcot in their respective pavilions as well.

While World Holiday Land was never built. perhaps some of the remaining ride ideas may get built but it is unlikely. The German skiing experience could be made in the Germany Pavilion as it already has an area that was to house a ride which never got built. So if they could get a sponsor it could be built but that is a long shot. It could add a thrill to the otherwise tame World Showcase.

Discovery Bay

Discovery Bay was originally planned to be an expansion to Frontierland. Frontierland was no longer popular with guests as it had been when it first opened with the rest of Disneyland. The popularity of Davy Crockett had faded and so had the popularity of Frontierland. A whole new section would be designed by a new generation of Imagineers. Discovery Bay was the idea of Tony Baxter who had only recently joined Imagineering. While he may have been new, he had the help of many experienced Imagineers such as Claude Coats and Marc Davis. Eventually, Discovery Bay would outgrow Frontierland and become a land in its own right.

Discovery Bay would first be announced in the Disney annual stock report. This is one of those times a land got very close. Official announcements were made public, lots of concept art was made, and models were made. Discovery Bay was even featured in a preview center on Main Street. Disney put a large amount of time , money, and effort into Discovery Bay.

Between the front of Frontierland and the front of Discovery Bay would be a mine train roller coaster. This would create a transition between the old and new Frontierland. Where the roller coasters would actually end up, Frontierland or Discovery Bay, is unclear. At various times it likely changed hands and may have done so in the real world like Matterhorn which would spend time as officially part of Tomorrowland as well as spending most of its time as a Fantasyland attraction.

The concept behind Discovery Bay was an alternate version of San Francisco in the decades that followed the gold rush. The design would be what we would now call steam punk, but this was many years before steam punk existed. It was similar in concept to the Jules Verne-inspired Tomorrowland, a land that might have been.

A lighthouse would be the wienie of the land to lure people in. The sailing ship *Columbia* would be converted to a play structure for kids to play on and have fun exploring. As in the real San Francisco Discovery Bay, there would be a Chinatown. This Chinatown would have a restaurant as well as a fireworks-themed shooting gallery which would expand into an interactive dark ride which will be discussed in more depth later.

There would be a re-creation of the *Nautilus* from *20,000 Leagues Under the Sea*. The *Nautilus* would not be just for show but would also include a walk-through attraction. Besides the walk-through there would also be a simulator ride which was to be called Captain Nemo's Adventure. Finally, there would be a luxury restaurant on board as well.

There would be a show that was planned to be in a revolving theater that would be known as Professor Marvel's Gallery of Wonders. Professor Marvel would show off his animals, experiments, and his inventions. Following the professor through the show would be his own personal small pet dragon that would perch on his shoulder like a parrot.

Another ride that was planned was the Western Balloon Ascent. This would have been a second version of the Skyway but it would go from Discovery Bay to another planned but never built land to be called Dumbo's Circusland. It may have gone through a glass-walled area that may have sent it through various scenes before going to Dumbo's Circusland.

Another airship-based ride would have been the main E-ticket attraction of the land. A hangar with the airship *Hyperion* sticking out would have featured an attraction called The Island at the Top of the World. The ride would have taken guests on a flying ship to an island at the top of the world. It is likely that this was to be a dark ride and not a simulator ride as some may have guessed it may have been, as the technology was not developed yet.

Not only had all of this been planned, but they even had second phase plans underway as well. The second phase would have featured the Spark Gap Coaster which would have been a small family friendly coaster. Another roller coaster was planned as well, simply known as the Tower.

Beyond the hangar to the Island at the Top of the World would be a large volcano, home of the Voyage Thru Time based on the H.G. Wells book *The Time Machine*. Another ride that was proposed for the expansion would have been both indoors as well as outdoors. This ride would have been known as the Lost World and would have featured a boat ride with dinosaurs long before Universal ever had one.

With some much planned and even announced, it may seem odd that it would never be built. A few problems led to the demise of the project. The first problem was that the movie *The Island at the Top of the World* did not do well at the box office and that was to be the main attraction of the first phase of Discovery Bay. Another major problem was the creation of Epcot and Tokyo Disneyland at the same time. With these projects Disney not only had money but also talent tied up in these other projects and could not spare people or money for a third project.

Other factors also may have contributed to the demise of Discovery Land. During the same time taste in film changed with science fiction becoming very popular. Disney would try to get involved with the genre with such films as *The Black Hole*. When Disney couldn't make its own successful science-fiction franchise they reached out to one of the most popular such franchises, *Star Wars*, and created Star Tours.

The concept of the Western Balloon Ascent was part of early plans for Epcot's Land Pavilion, but a new sponsor wanted a change in direction for the pavilion.

Epcot fans will probably have figured out the first idea that Discovery Bay originated but actually was built. Mr. Marvel would eventually become Figment and the Dreamfinder from Journey into Imagination.

Discoveryland would get its style from Discovery Bay. Many visual features would be included, such as the *Nautilus* and the *Hyperion* airship. The *Nautilus* walk-through would make it into the land. Plans were even made to include some of the Discovery Bay phase two rides including the Spark Gap roller coaster and the Tower. These were also phase 2 plans for Discoveryland and as Disneyland Paris did not do as well as expected, most phase 2 plans never were realized.

The new Tomorrowland would be inspired stylistically by Discovery Bay and more directly Discoveryland. It did not live up to Discoveryland and was far from what Discovery Bay could have been.

DisneySea would also have a similar feel in its Mysterious Island. But that is not the only thing that DisneySea borrowed from Discover Bay. DisneySea's Fortress Explorations also features a ship for kids to explore much like Discovery Bay was to have.

The one ride that you probably guessed did make it to Disneyland and even around the world was the mine train which we now know as Thunder Mountain. It was Thunder Mountain's connection to Discovery Bay which is why Disneyland's version is the one version of the ride that is based on Bryce Canyon instead of Monument Valley like the other Thunder Mountains around the world.

With the creation of a Star Wars Land in the area that was once going to have Discovery Bay, it is unlikely that Discovery Bay will become a land any time soon. With land at a premium, it is very unlikely that if it were made it would be made in Disneyland. However, it is possible that some of the ideas will get into other attractions as they have already done.

Dumbo's Circusland

As we already mentioned, Dumbo's Circusland was being planned at the same time as Discovery Bay. Also as already mentioned, a Western Balloon Ascent ride would connect the two lands.

Dumbo's Circusland was to be located next to It's a Small World. It would have been inside as well as outside of the berm.

The land would have housed a Dumbo ride, but this time Dumbo would be elevated giving a more thrilling ride. A dark ride for Pinocchio would once more be planned. Mickey's Madhouse would have given Mickey his own dark ride, something that seems to be very much needed. Alice has a dark ride, a tea party, a cottage in the Storybook Land Canals, and is in It's a Small World, yet all Mickey gets is a house. How did Alice get so much love and Mickey get so little?

The main attraction of Dumbo's Circusland would be Circus Disney which was to be another dark ride. This ride would have seen Disney characters as audio animatronics. The ride would feature wild animals where you would see some of the cast of *The Jungle Book*, and you would go through the sideshow and see characters such as Horace Horsecollar, the Reluctant Dragon, and Dumbo. The ride's finale would be in the

Big Top where you would see a three-ring show including the Flying Goofy's.

Dumbo's Circusland would have only taken up 5 acres. It would have freed up some land in Fantasyland where the Dumbo ride was located. It not only had concept art drawn up, it also had models of the overall ride and even maquettes for the Circus Disney were made. Yet it would never get built.

The same reasons Discovery Bay never were built led to the demise of Dumbo's Circusland. It is possible that between the two lands most find Discovery Bay to be the more exciting land, but Dumbo's Circusland may have been cheaper to build so may have had an advantage if it came down to money. Also, a ride featuring Mickey is just screaming to be made.

While Dumbo's Circusland never was built, some of the ideas would make it into the park. The most obvious is Pinocchio's Daring Journey. A new version of Dumbo would be built and moved to a different location, but it would not be elevated but simply placed on the ground. Audio-animatronic Disney cartoon figures would get a show at Disney World known as the Mickey Mouse Revue. This show would then move to Tokyo Disneyland. Some of the concept art for the land would also get displayed in the Disneyland Hotel in the Bonita Tower lobby.

Perhaps someday some of the concepts will resurface. It would be great to see some classic Disney characters brought to life as audio animatronics. It would especially be nice to see both classic characters such as Mickey get the respect they deserve, but it would be nice to see other characters like Horace Horsecollar and the Reluctant Dragon also get some love.

Tomorrowland 2055

Tomorrowland 2055 was to be an updated version of Tommorowland. While we would get an updated version eventually, most Disney fans that know about the two different versions would easily choose to have Tomorrowland 2055 over the version we got.

The Tomorrowland 2055 has a backstory that while doing some work at the park some crystals were uncovered. These crystals sent a message to space which brought aliens to Earth to visit the park. A new nighttime parade known as the Lightkeepers which was a planned parade to replace the Main Street Electrical Parade was part of the expansion and would have included the alien backstory.

One of the main attractions that was to be added was Alien Encounter. Initially, Disney owned the rights to the alien from the movie *Alien* and planned to use that as the alien, but some Imagineers thought that it would be to scary. There was debate over it and the Imagineers got George Lucas to convince Michael Eisner that it was too scary for Disney. The ride may have gotten made before the Florida version, but it took so long that Florida made their version first and when it was made they had to scale it back because it was too scary. With the problems with Disney World, the Alien Encounter idea was dropped completely for Disneyland.

Another attraction that was planned to be built in the Carousel Theater which at the time was unused was to be an audio-animatronic alien musical show. A few different versions were proposed. More will be discussed later, but each version Michael Eisner did not like so changes were made but nothing ever got his approval.

A 360-degree film with animatronics was also planned. This was just an import of Timekeeper. Rocket Rods also was going to be more thrilling with sponsorship from GM who would handle the expense of creating a new track system. When that fell through, Disney just kept the old PeopleMover system which infamously was part of the reason Rocket Rods never was able to do well, as the ride needed more room to get speed.

Overall, more money was initially planned for the area, but cutbacks were continually made and what we ended up with was the current version of Tomorrowland. While money was a problem, like so many other failed projects Tomorrowland 2055 had other issues. The problems with Alien Encounter during the whole process took out an important new part of the land. Michael Eisner never being able to find an audio-animatronic alien show idea he liked ended one of the other parts of the plan. After losing most of what kept the back story intact, there was little left of a coherent story to explain the changes.

While Alien Encounter was initially going to get placed in Tomorrowland 2055, it took too long for the project to be started and instead it ended up at Walt Disney World. Even with all the changes it was plagued with problems of being too scary for children and finally was modified with Stitch as the main character in the show. Lightkeepers would be the inspiration for the short-lived Light Magic.

Hollywoodland

Hollywoodland would be the last land developed for Disneyland that would not get built. When

Disney-MGM Studios was first built, it was a huge success. The new park ushered in what would be referred to as the Disney Decade. Unfortunately, not all projects would have such success and failed projects as you have seen such as Disneyland Paris would end many plans. The success of the then-named Disney-MGM Studios was the inspiration for a land at Disneyland which would be named Hollywoodland.

The area would be themed to 1930s-40s Hollywood. It would be located behind Space Mountain so plans were made to change the back side of Space Mountain into the Hollywood Hills which would probably include the Hollywoodland sign with the original land section intact as opposed to the current Hollywood sign.

The main attraction would be Dick Tracy's Crime Stoppers which we will look at in more depth later. Other rides would have included the Toontown Trolley not as we know it now but as a simulator. More information will be discussed later about this attraction. Baby Herman's Runaway Buggy Ride would have been another dark ride which we will mention later. The Great Movie Ride would be brought over from Florida, but due to size some changes may have been made although we may have gotten some updates as well. Finally, Superstar Television, another import, from Florida would be included.

This is another example of things not working out because of the Euro Disneyland failure, although other factors helped the demise as well. For instance, Disney wanted to push Roger Rabbit as the next Mickey. While Roger was popular for a time, with Roger Rabbit merchandise being hard to find as it would sell out, Roger never had the impact Michael Eisner had hoped for and was just a temporary fad. With two majors rides built around Roger, the land didn't have much going for it. The failure of Dick Tracy to be as successful as had been hoped along with other problems we will mention later also took out another big attraction in the land.

The only thing to make it into another park was the name, and even that saw some changes. With the theme being 1930's Hollywood, all the material in it has Hollywoodland written as one word while the California Adventures area is Hollywood Land.

Star Wars Land

You probably already heard about the new Star Wars Land coming, but this is an earlier concept. It would not be a full land so much as another Tomorrowland makeover. It is also only a rumor with no known concept art in existence, but it is a rumor that persisted for some time and aspects of it did get into the park, so there is likely some truth to the rumors.

A speeder bike ride was planned possibly for the old PeopleMover track. Near Autopia would be an Ewok village. A *Millennium Falcon* walk-through would be put where the old PeopleMover loading area had been. The Astro Orbiter was to be moved near Space Mountain. A cantina restaurant show would also be added.

Most likely this is one of those times an idea got improved upon. Instead of a make over for Tomorrowland, *Star Wars* would get its own land.

Tomorrowland would get some *Star Wars* added, with Space Mountain getting a makeover and some other additions. Some of these ideas are probably going to make it into the new Star Wars Land. But we will have to wait until it is built to know for sure.

Walt Disney World: Magic Kingdom

Surprisingly, the Magic Kingdom has had little planned that has not been built that the public knows about. The reason could be that unlike Disneyland the Orlando park did not get created from scratch but took the blueprint from Disneyland and worked with that.

Thunder Mesa

Thunder Mesa was an area that would feature a mine train roller coaster, pack mule ride, and canoes, as well as a massive dark ride.

The Western River Expedition was the main ride for the area. The ride was going to be the Magic Kingdom's answer to the Pirates of the Caribbean, since Disney felt with real pirates closer to Florida no one would be interested in fake ones. Guests continued to demand the Pirate ride and that would replace the Western River Expedition. Without its main attraction, the land itself was left on the drawing board.

Many ideas have come out of the Thunder Mesa area such as the mine train ride which would even feature a backwards section that would end up becoming a part of Expedition Everest. Disneyland Paris would take the name for its version of Frontierland.

Shadowlands

Shadowlands was going to be a land based on the Disney villains. The initial idea for Shadowlands was based on an idea for a villains ride for the Magic Kingdom which will be discussed later. The ride developed into a whole land.

The land would feature the original ride that created the land idea. Besides the main attraction, other rides would also have been in the land such as an Ursula spinner ride.

The idea was so good it was decided to upgrade it to a full park. However, being a full park means it takes more money and is less likely to be built.

The Ursula spinner idea keeps coming back as we will see later so the ideas of the ride are still in the minds of the Imagineers and it is possible that some of them may make it into a park someday.

Epcot: World Showcase

Epcot was a visionary idea that Walt had. Epcot may not have been practical for even Walt, and had he lived he may have not be able to pull off such a bold project. However, once Walt died no one really knew how to make Epcot. The company wanted to fulfill the late founder's dream, but did not know how.

So the best that the Disney company could come up with was to make a World Fair of sorts. Like other World Fairs there would be pavilions sponsored by corporations as well as pavilions sponsored by countries. Unlike world fairs with everything mixed up, Disney would separate things between countries and companies.

As you will see, most of the lost lands of Epcot were country pavilions that Disney would try to get sponsor to pay for. Disney was happy to make a pavilion for any country that wanted one badly enough to pay for it. If a country showed interest, Disney would work out some ideas and some concept art. In some cases, Disney would come close to making a deal with a country only for it to fall apart before finally going through. Little is know about some of these pavilions as they probably did not get far into development. Often, if a country showed any interest Disney was ready to work on a possible pavilion.

Another problem that would plague some of the countries were political issues which would change during the development of the park. The park took quite a long time to build and the world could change a great deal during that time.

While countries are the majority of the lands that never made it into Epcot, there were a couple other pavilions that would have been placed in the Future World section. These lost pavilions would fare much better with one going on to inspire an entire new park. The other would not get made at first, but would see its theme made even though many of the ideas from the original plan for the theme would not make it.

Arab Nations Pavilion

Disney tried to get a pavilion with a country from the Middle East. As it was becoming hard to get anyone to sign up, they thought they would make it easier by getting multiple countries in a region to split the cost. This was a method you will see they used with other regions as well.

There were similarities to the other Middle East pavilions they have been working on. This pavilion would feature a bazaar. The second floor would feature a circular restaurant possibly giving you a glimpse of the pavilion's ride like you can get at The Land. The big draw of the pavilion would be a magic carpet ride. The ride would have some interesting special effects with a genie. It would take you through a history of the region's influence on science and architecture.

While the Arab Nations Pavilion never got made, one of the countries Disney was trying to get to back it did get on board and ultimately would get their own pavilion. Some of the ideas such as the bazaar would live on in the Morocco Pavilion.

Australia Pavilion

Being an entire continent gives you some clout. Little is known about this land. There is speculation that a Sydney Opera House re-creation would be used in some way. A model was made which features what appears to be Sydney Opera House which may confirm that this was the case.

Costa Rica Pavilion

The Costa Rica Pavilion was just one of many country pavilions that could have made it into Epcot. The pavilion would have housed a crystal building which would have housed tropical plants and waterfalls. Local foods would have been sold along with traditional arts and crafts. The buildings would have been in the Spanish Colonial architectural style. Like many Epcot attractions it just never happened.

Denmark Pavilion

Denmark actually came very close to sponsoring a pavilion at Epcot. The pavilion would have been indoors and featured a re-creation of Tivoli Gardens, one of the inspirations for Disneyland; a Ferris wheel (something Walt did not want in one of his parks), and a carousel. The main attraction would have been a LEGO-themed boat ride.

While Denmark did not make it, Scandinavia did get representation with the Norway Pavilion. While Disney would not get a LEGO-themed boat ride Legoland, would make their own in their own park much later.

Equatorial Africa Pavilion

With few African countries with the resources to to be sponsor, a pavilion for the entire area was instead thought of. The pavilion was to have a treehouse. There would be a show as well. The pavilion went as far as getting models made. While the concept never got off the drawing board, aspects of the pavilion would help lead to Animal Kingdom.

Iran Pavilion

Iran would have had a bazaar much like the Morocco Pavilion. What would make Iran stand out would be an entire dark ride through the history of Persia.

With oil money and a pro-western government, it is likely that Iran would easily have been able and even willing to pay to sponsor a pavilion. The reason it never was built was that the Shah was overthrown before the park was being built and after that the chances of an Iran Pavilion are slim to none.

However, some aspects of the pavilion may appear again and some have in some small way. The bazaar would appear in the Morocco Pavilion and some other Epcot scenes such as in Spaceship Earth would feature Middle Eastern history for a brief moment.

Israel Pavilion

The Israel Pavilion came very close to getting built and opening with the park. They were featured as a future attraction in some of the literature and even had a large sign featuring concept art declaring the pavilion would be built on a particular spot in the park.

The pavilion was to be a re-creation of ancient Jerusalem. It was to have a stage and an open air restaurant. It was to have a minaret as an information kiosk and small stalls similar to the bazaar ideas of other locations.

While it came close, financing ended up falling through and concerns were made about it becoming a possible terrorist target.

Mexico Pavilion

Yes, there is a Mexico Pavilion already, but it is not what it could have been. Originally, there would have been a different entrance featuring a talking Olmec statue like the one found in the pavilion. The boats would have been flower boats more in line with the tradition and culture of Mexico. The ride itself would have covered more of the history of Mexico with many famous people from Mexico's history such as Father Hidalgo, Benito Juarez, Pancho Villa, and Emeliano Zapata. The inside was also planned to be more elaborate.

While the current Mexico Pavilion did not live up to the plans, it still was able to get made and gave us one of the few World Showcase pavilions that has a ride.

Philippines Pavilion

The Philippines Pavilion was one of the first pavilions that Disney worked on. The reason that it got such special treatment was the ambassador had expressed great interest in the project. There would be a show about the Philippines that would be shown over a large area bigger then a normal single screen. It appears that a restaurant would also be in the middle of the show so you could eat while you watched. Also planned would be a stage for live performances. Finally, some shopping was planned for the pavilion.

While the ambassador was interested, once First Lady Imelda Marcos learned how much it cost she first probably thought she could buy a lot of shoes with the money, but she said that it was too much money for a country like the Philippines, and if it had that much money it would spend it on schools, hospital, and other such improvements.

Puerto Rico Pavilion

The Puerto Rico Pavilion has had very little information come out about it. It is one of many pavilions that little information is available on. One thing that has been said is that it would have been part of the phase 2 expansion.

Scandinavia Pavilion

While Disney tried to get Denmark to join, they knew they wanted a Nordic country. Disney decided that it might be easier to get multiple countries to come together to pay for a pavilion so they decided to try to get countries interested in a Scandinavia theme requiring less from each country. The only country that was interested was Norway, which eventually got its very own pavilion and did not have to share.

Soviet Union Pavilion

This may be one of the strangest pavilions ever planned. It was to be a pavilion about a communist country in one of the most capitalistic of all locations in the world. St. Basils was to be the main architectural landmark. The pavilion would feature a show named "Russia The Bells of Change." The show would feature animatronics, live actors, and film telling the history of the country.

What lead to the pavilion's downfall was the downfall of the Soviet Union. With no Soviet Union there was no pavilion. It is unfortunate that a sponsor could not be found for this pavilion to be made into a Russia Pavilion. The Soviet Union may have seen it as a chance to show off and at the time the Cold War had been in a thawing-off period before the final end.

Spain Pavilion

Spain was another pavilion that got so far as to get its own billboard and mention in various printed media. Spain might have become one of the best pavilions. As most pavilions have at most a show and only a few can claim to have a ride, Spain would be the only pavilion to feature a ride and a show. The ride would have been a boat ride featuring the culture of Spain. The film would have featured the history of Spain. There would also have been a restaurant.

Switzerland Pavilion

The Switzerland Pavilion would have brought the Matterhorn to Disney World. It appears a Swiss village would have been built at the base. It would have likely featured shops and a restaurant featuring local food. The main attraction of the Switzerland Pavilion, though, would be the Matterhorn ride. It is said that it would have been an updated version but that was in the 1980s, so it probably would be behind the latest version at Disneyland.

The Switzerland Pavilion was being negotiated with the Swiss government. When that fell through attempts were made to find corporate sponsors, but they could not be found. One thing that I like about Disneyland is that it does have the Matterhorn and no one else. It gives Disneyland something special.

United Arab Emirates Pavilion

The United Arab Emirates Pavilion would have been another unique pavilion. It would feature not only a ride but also a show. The ride would be a magic carpet ride through the Arab world. The show would talk about Middle Eastern contributions to science.

Perhaps this fell through for the same reason Israel did. It may have been viewed as a possible terrorist target. Or perhaps there were problems deciding how to handle a carpet ride through the Arab world as many of the sites at the time would probably be of a religious nature such as Mecca. With oil money floating around it would seem that money would not have been a major problem.

United States Pavilion

While the U.S. did get a pavilion there were some ideas for the pavilion that never made it into the real world. Even the show that did get made had many changes including removing Will Rogers as a main narrator when it was decided too few people knew who he was. Tom and Huck also didn't make it, but the raft they were to use did.

The first project suggested was a boat ride which was inspired by the Western River Expedition. This ride would use song and folk legends to tell the tale of the U.S. Paul Bunyan would make an appearance and possibly other American folk legends like Johnny Appleseed and Pecos Bill. With the musical theme it may have been similar to Disneyland's America Sings.

This is one instance where cost or lack of a sponsor did not kill the plans for a project. What sunk the boat ride was that Disney wanted to take a more serious approach and decided to go with the show they have today.

Venezuela Pavilion

The Venezuela Pavilion was another pavilion that was announced. It was going to have an aerial tram through a rain forest where guests would search for El Dorado the Lost City of Gold. It would have also had a modern high rise to show Venezuela's modernity. A statue of Simon Bolivar was also going to be prominently featured.

The deal fell through and South America would not have a place in the World Showcase. Mexico would be the closest they would get. It is possible that having a boat ride in the same park that also went through a rainforest may have been a problem as well.

New Zealand Pavilion

Little is known about plans for New Zealand. It is one of a number of countries invited to a special presentation held at Disney World prior to building the park.

Romania Pavilion

Little information is known about plans for Romania. What is known is that it was one of the invited guests to the first presentation given to countries about the park.

Greece Pavilion

Greece is another country that little information is known about. The only thing known was it was invited to the first presentation offered to various countries on the World Showcase project.

Brazil Pavilion

Little is known about the Brazil pavilion. The only information is that the initial design work for the pavilion was done by Imagineer Claude Coats.

This was another instance of money not being found for the project. For years rumors would persist that this would be the next land added. However, the rumors never ended up being true.

Poland Pavilion

The Poland Pavilion is known to have been a possible addition as art for it was displayed at an Art of Disney exhibition. Besides this one time, there is little other evidence to show us what this pavilion would have been like.

Epcot: Future World

As we mentioned at the start of the Epcot section, most of the land projects that would not get built at Epcot would be country pavilions. However, there were also some Future World pavilions that would not make it into Epcot.

Future World did undergo many changes during its time. Most pavilions had multiple ideas that were created for each pavilion. One reason that so many versions were created which would lead to rides that would not be built was that they were working with corporate sponsors. One sponsor may fall through and another would come on board. Many sponsors wanted changes made to the pavilions. However, with the number of large companies being greater than countries, and many of these companies having more money than many countries, it was not as hard to get pavilions made.

Disney also had a smaller number of ideas for Future World pavilions. The following two pavilions did not make it to Epcot on opening day, but both would end up in Orlando in one way or another.

Movie Pavilion

For our look at the unrealized Epcot pavilions we have one that is not part of the World Showcase. The park was originally planned to have a Movie Pavilion. The pavilion would feature a ride which would take guests through scenes from classic Hollywood films. If this sounds familiar, it should be. The story of the Movie Pavilion is a story of when an idea gets lucky and not only gets built but expanded upon.

The idea for the Movie Pavilion would not only end up being made much as it was planned, but it would inspire an entire park. The idea for the Movie Pavilion became The Great Movie Ride. The ride would inspire the creation of Disney-MGM Studios.

Space Pavilion

The Space Pavilion was not one of the original pavilions planned for the park. It was planned in the early 1990s. The Space Pavilion would have taken the place of the Horizons ride. When entering the pavilion you would be outside and get to a campfire-like setting where you would experience a pre-show with lights and sounds in the sky. Next you would enter the pavilion's version of the hydrolator; instead of going to the bottom of the sea, it would take you to outer space. The pavilion would have a hands-on area. The main draw would be the spacewalk which would allow you to control the yaw and roll but not pitch.

The Imagineers were limited by the Disney accountants. They needed to use the Horizons building instead of removing it because they would not be able depreciate the building cost of the current building if a new one was made. They planned to take the system that was already in place and make some changes to allow for the Spacewalk experience. They also wanted to have a shuttle experience to take you back to Earth when you left the building, but Disney decided that would be an unnecessary cost and guests would simply leave the building from space right into Epcot.

At this point you probably see one main problem was money. There already was a ride in the space and to change anything would cost money. If money was to be spent to change the attraction, Disney wanted to spend as little as possible. The limitations made it difficult for the Imagineers to create the experience they wanted. Restrictive requirements of having to use the pre-existing building also made things difficult.

Once Horizons had fully been depreciated and had no sponsor, it could be torn down. That is what happened. While it may seem that Mission:SPACE was a modern version of the Space Pavilion, one Imagineer who spoke anonymously said none of the same Imaginers were involved in the two projects so the only real link is the location and space being involved. However, it is possible that some on the project had been at Disney at the time and heard about it or had gone through the archives and seen something about the project. Even fans such as myself have seen some concept art so it is not hard to imagine that some Imagineers may have as well. But the two projects are very different from one another. It is possible that the Space Pavilion had some small impact on Mission:SPACE, but it seems that Mission:SPACE was mostly its own creation.

Weather Pavilion

The Weather Pavilion was planned to be made with the help of the Weather Chanel. The pavilion would teach guests about weather prediction, meteorology, and broadcasting. Computers would show the weather in guests' home towns. The move would have brought at least some of the Weather Channel broadcast to Epcot. Not only was the Weather Channel in talks with Disney ,the National Hurricane Center was also in talks to get involved with the pavilion.

Disney's Hollywood Studios

When Disney's Hollywood Studios first opened as Disney-MGM Studios, it was very popular. With the popularity of the park a few expansion ideas were planned. The park would see some expansion and will soon see many changes soon. But these ideas were left in the dust. With the initial popularity of the park money would not be an issue with any of these expansions. All the lands that went unbuilt in the park were not made for various reasons besides economic ones.

Mickey's Movieland

Mickey's Movieland was to be a replica of the original Disney Hyperion Avenue studio. Mickey's Movieland would have been located where Sunset Boulevard is now. The main attraction of the land would be a show that would showcase how cartoons are made. The land would also have displays of various cartoon-making equipment. The land may have had some kind of hands-on exhibits allowing guests to experience movie making.

The main reason that this land was never built was because another project took its place. The current Sunset Boulevard with the Hollywood Tower of Terror would understandably get the spot instead in an attempt to bring more thrills into the park.

While Mickey's Movieland may not have been made, parts of it would go on to make it into other areas of the Disney parks. The Magic of Disney Animation would take the idea of showing guests how animation is made. In California Adventure, the Disney Animation attraction includes a similar show about animation called Animation Academy. Also at the Disney Animation attraction the Sorcerer's Workshop has hands-on experiences like making your own simple animation and dubbing a film.

Muppet Studios

The Muppet Studios was an area that was planned and was known at other times as Muppet Movieland. The land was planned to be opened in two phases. The land would include the Muppet*Vision movie that is currently shown in the park and in California Adventure. The second phase would feature a ride that would spoof The Great Movie Ride with animatronic Muppets as the main attraction for the second phase. The other main addition planned for phase two would be a zany restaurant featuring Gonzo as the owner.

The first phase did get completed enough for us to see the Muppet*Vision movie finished. However, the

Muppets would not get an entire land. During the planning phases, Disney was working with Jim Henson on a deal for the rights to the Muppets. Jim Henson would pass away before the deal could be signed. Henson had worked on the Muppet Vision movie and it was one of the last projects he was working on before his death. The film was completed without him.

With the tragic death of Jim Henson, the whole thing would fall through and a second phase would never be built. While an entire land dedicated to the Muppets would never be built, Muppet*Vision did make it and now entertains guests on both coasts.

Roger Rabbit's Hollywood

Roger Rabbit's Hollywood was the final proposed land for Disney's Hollywood Studios. The location for the proposed land is uncertain, with some claiming it would have been off of Sunset Boulevard and others claiming that it was to be a whole new area. What is known is that it would have been an East Coast version of Toontwon with three new rides and would focus on the world of Roger Rabbit over Mickey and his friends.

Three rides were planned for Roger Rabbit's Hollywood. The rides would be located inside Maroon Studios from the film *Who Framed Roger Rabbit?*. The rides would be Toontown Trolley, a simulator ride through Toontown; Benny the Cab, a dark ride; and Baby Herman's Runaway Baby Buggy. Besides the rides, Roger Rabbit's Hollywood would also feature a restaurant that would be like the bar in the film.

Two main factors contributed to Roger Rabbit's Hollywood never being built. The first problem was Disney had legal issues with Amblin over the rights to the character. The second problem was that Roger Rabbit did not stay as popular as they had hoped and they did not think the character warranted a whole new land.

While the land would not be built, Toontown at Disneyland would give us a glimpse of the world of toons and their home. Also in Toontown the Roger Rabbits Car Toon Spin was what the Benny the Cab ride would have been. While you may think it;s the Benny the Cab ride with a new name, you actually are riding Lenny the cab, a cousin of Benny's. The reason you ride Lenny and not Benny is Amblin does not have any right to the new character Lenny.

Tokyo Disneyland

Being located overseas and not directly owned by Disney, Tokyo Disneyland does not have as many projects that were planned for it. Typically Tokyo Disneyland gets what was planned for the U.S. Disney parks. Usually, they get older rides and sometimes make improvements on them such as the Winnie the Pooh ride which was improved for Tokyo. Other times rides that were planned for the U.S. parks such as Meet the World which was to be located in the Japan Pavilion get sent to Japan instead.

Entire lands are not as common. While money problems throughout the Disney empire such as the poor performance of Disneyland Paris may be a problem for other Disney parks, since Disney does not pay for the projects it is not a problem for them to make all the lands that the Oriental Land Company which owns the park want. This is another reason few ideas for lands fail to get made for the park. Just like in Anaheim,

Tokyo Disneyland has limited room so expansion is difficult as entire new lands require lots of space.

Mickey Ville

Mickey Ville was the first planned version for a Toontown. Howeve,r the theme would be much different. The plan was that Mickey Ville would have a medieval theme. At first this may sound odd but the idea was that it would be themed to *The Brave Little Tailor, Fun and Fancy Free*, and *Mickey and the Beanstalk*.

The area would feature houses of various Disney characters. Most would be the facade of a large theater that was to be built. Some would be actual areas to explore such as a house boat for Donald. The only ride that is known to have been planned was a small boat ride around a small river. There would be a couple of stores including a music store as well as a candy store that looked like it was made out of candy.

The reason Mickey Ville never made it was that the Oriental Land Company found out about another project that Disney was working on at the same time known as Toontown. They decided they would wait and see how this new land was received in the U.S. before continuing any development on Mickey Ville. With the success of Toontown, the Oriental Land Company decided they wanted to have Toontown placed in the spot planned for Mickey Ville instead. A good amount of the cost of a new land or ride is in the development, so having already spent that money on Toontown it freed up money for the new land that Mickey Ville would have needed for its development as well as additional time needed to create and build something that only had just begun.

While Mickey Ville seems to have started first, it did not get developed as quickly as Toontown. It may have offered some limited inspiration for Toontown, but it is likely that it was only a small amount. It has yet to see its few ideas make it out into the real world.

Sci-Fi City

Sci-Fi City was not going to be a totally new land but an update of Tomorowland. This update is considered by many to have been the most ambitious plan ever made for a Tomorrowland improvement. Besides some outside changes, Star Tours and the Honey I Shrunk the Audience shows would remain the same; the rest of the area would be upgraded. Space Mountain would become Hyper Space mountain with some upgrades such as on-ride audio and new show elements. A version of Rocket Rods would have transported guests around the area. The Rocket Jets would have become saucers. A new area known as Crater Town would have featured a Space Pirate Hideout inspired by the film *Treasure Planet* that had not yet been released. The Grand Prix would have become a lunar rover ride. One whole new attraction would have been an animatronic aliens with a big show at the end.

The whole place was inspired by movies and other media. The theme would have been a science-fiction world that never was but borrowed from many famous science-fiction films and shows from the last century.

The main reason the plan was rejected by the Oriental Land Company was cost. The company had already been putting a large amount of money into DisneySea. Other problems include the issues with the U.S. version of Rocket Rods making them not want to use the same ride. A lack of knowledge of how well the film *Treasure Planet* would do was another concern for that part of the plan. Had the plan been presented at another time, it may have at least seen parts of it make it, but presenting it to the company when they were already underway on a large, ambitious project made it unlikely to ever get the green light.

The name Hyperspace Mountain would be used. The updated and improvements to Space Mountain would also be used in other parks. However, little else of what might have been a fun, exciting take on Tomorrowland has made it into the Disney parks.

Peter Pan Miniland

Little is know about the Peter Pan Miniland. One piece of concept art is known to exist. In the concept art, we see buildings which may have been planned to house a dark ride. A store called Hook's Treasure Chest would be in the land. The land would feature a pirate ship in a lagoon with a large crocodile statute and a mermaid statue.

With such little information, it is hard to tell why this miniland never was made. It is also hard to tell if any part of the land made it into other parks.

Disneyland Paris

Being only partially owned by Disney is one reason that Disneyland Paris has not seen many lands that did not get made. Being overseas and not in the U.S. is another reason new lands are not as likely to be thought up for Disneyland Paris, which means they are less likely to have lands that do not get made. While the financial problems facing the park would seem to be the likely problem for these lands, only half of the lands did not get built because of the financial difficulties caused by the park.

1920s Main Street

1920s Main Street was planned as a possible replacement for Main Street, U.S.A. While it would have been roughly the same, the theme and time would have been different. It would have been a more modern version of Main Street circa the 1920s. Some of the new stores and attractions would include Capone's, a jazz club; Nighthawks Dinner; the Dark Room, a camera shop; Marconi's, which would focus on the 20's fascination with radio; a gas station; and Cone Shop, an ice cream shop.

1920s Main Street would feature the standard attractions seen at other Main Streets at other Disney parks such as a train station, a city hall, and an opera house.

The downfall of 1920s Main Street was simple, as Disney decided that they should stick to the traditional Main Street. Cost was not going to be a major issue as it would have been similar in price to build as the Main Street which was built. It just came down to preference.

Indiana Jones land

The Indiana Jones land was going to be a miniland that would have been an expansion to the park. The land was to have a mine car roller coaster along with its own version of the Indiana Jones Adventure as seen in Disneyland in Anaheim and Tokyo Disneyland. Unlike Disneyland, where it is located in a land, the Indiana Jones land would be an entire small land of its own.

The financial troubles that Disneyland Paris suffered early on are the reason that this land was never built. The Indiana Jones ride was a very expensive ride and the cost would have been high to make the ride and the land.

While the Indiana Jones land was never made, half of the attractions were made. The mine train roller coaster was built. The Indiana Jones Adventure was built, but it was not original to the Indiana Jones land and the ride creation predates the land so the Indiana Jones land did not influence it.

Disney's Animal Kingdom

Disney's Animal Kingdom is already the largest theme park in the world. This may sound odd, especially if you have ever visited the park, but the reason is the area used for the animals which require such large space. The safari ride is the largest ride of all. So the park has lots of room which would allow it to expand. From the very outset plans were made for a second phase expansion which would never materialize.

The park did see some small expansions such as the Asia section and soon will have a new Avatar land. However, this being a park with animals, the hours are limited. The limited hours may play a factor in limiting the expansion or where the park can expand. Another factor that limits the number of new lands that never got built for Animal Kingdom is that the park is the newest of all the parks on Walt Disney World property so there has not been as much time for new lands to be thought up for the park. Also there are now more parks that Disney has to worry about than when only one or two parks took up the company's time.

Beastly Kingdom

Beastly Kingdom was going to be located where Camp Mickey-Minnie was placed and where Avatar land will soon be located. Animal Kingdom initially was to have animals that are extinct, living, and mythic. The logo of Animal Kingdom features all three kinds of animals including a dragon. Signs of mythological creatures can still be found in various locations of the park. An example of mythological creatures include a unicorn section of the parking lot. A dragon is one of the animals that are featured in the ticket booth reminding guests of what might have been had Beastly Kingdom been made. The only mythological creature currently in the park is the Yeti and soon Avatar will include make-believe aliens, too.

Beastly Kingdom would have been divided into two sections, one good and one evil. The good section would have featured a maze that was to be called Quest of the Unicorn. The maze would have ended in a grotto where you would find an animatronic unicorn. Fantasia Gardens would have been a boat ride through scenes from the animated film *Fantasia*.

The main attraction for the evil section would have been the roller coaster Dragon's Tower. The ride would have you enlisted by some bats to help steal the treasure of a dragon. The end would have you face the dragon itself.

At one point during the development of the park, it was decided that this land would have to be put off until a second phase. The two lands that were being considered to be dropped from the initial opening were DinoLand USA or Beastly Kingdom. Disney ultimately decided that it would include DinoLand USA in its opening phase and Beastly Kingdom would have to wait for a second phase. Disney planned to build an inexpensive place holder area, Camp Mickey-Minnie, to have something in the spot until they began the second phase expansion.

Animal Kingdom opened and it was successful. However, Disney decided they did not want to invest the money that would be necessary to add a whole new land. Instead, they slowly added to Asia with rides like Kali River Rapids opening and eventually Expedition Everest.

While none of the plans for Beastly Kingdom have ever made it into a Disney theme park, they may have made it into another Orlando theme park. It is said that some of the Imagineers who worked on the project left Disney and went to work for Universal. The Dragon Tower is believed to have become the Dueling Dragons which would later be turned into Dragon Challenge. However, much of the story elements of the bats enlisting guests and trying to steal the dragon's gold would be removed along with the animatronic dragon. This story is very popular among Beastly Kingdom fans but understandably has not been confirmed.

Australia

An Australia section of the park has long been talked about. Before the park even opened, an idea was to make a reproduction of the Ayers Rocks and put the animals there. While Animal Kingdom was long thought to need more to make the park a full-day destination, Australia was always a good choice. The unusual animals lend themselves to the park.

At times Australia had a good chance. However, Animal Kingdom has been working on making itself a full-day park. With Avatar land it is unlikely they will do much more to Animal Kingdom in the near future. In time Australia may still get a spot in Animal Kingdom. It may not be as exciting as Beastly Kingdom, but it would be a cheaper, more practical option.

Disney California Adventure

There are a number of reasons that Disney California Adventure only has a few proposed lands which were never built. One is there is little room in the area to expand. Another is that the park has not seen many expansion plans that never made it past the development stage is because it is a newer park and it will likely see more plans in the future that will go unrealized.

Carland

You might think that I made a spelling error, but no, I mean Carland not Carsland. From the very beginning Carland was on the drawing board for Disney California Adventure. What is more Californian than cars? It fit with the park's concept perfectly. The land would have one main ride which will be discussed in more detail later. The main ride would have been a car ride to see some crazy tourist traps.

Like the whole Disney California Adventure in general, budget concerns were certainly an issue that kept this land from happening. However, the biggest concern was a lack of Disney properties that fit the theme. Disney wanted merchandise they could sell. Herbie would be the best fit, but Herbie is not as popular as he once was.

While Carland never got made, it was a popular idea with Imagineers and executives. Once the movie *Cars* became a success, Disney finally had something they could market that fit in with the theme. Carland would ultimately become Carsland. While Carsland would make changes to Carland to fit with the franchise, it used Carland and some of its ideas as a seed of an idea for some of the land and rides.

Toy Story Pier

Toy Story Pier was planned for the Disney California Adventure expansion. Most of the plans would be simple refurbishments and face lifts to already existing rides. The only real new change would be Toy Story Midway Mania.

While the idea of giving Paradise Pier a face lift did ultimately come to fruition, giving it a Toy Story theme did not. The only Toy Story Pier attraction to make it was the Toy Story Midway Mania which was always a fairly sure thing.

Ultimately, Disney decided that it would have had too much Toy Story and decided the Toy Story Pier was not a great idea. Most likely it realized that to add another full land dedicated to a Pixar franchise would have turned Disney California Adventure into Pixar Place. Had they made the changes it would have made the entrance of Buena Vista Street and Pacific Wharf the only areas untouched by Pixar, and those are barely lands. It would also mean an entire three lands would be completely based on Pixar films.

Monsters Inc.

A Monsters Inc. Miniland which had been planed as a possible Hollywood Studios addition was planned to be moved to California Adventures. There is almost no information about the Hollywood Studios version, so we will just talk about the California version.

The changes would have been minimal. Most of them would be to facades to create a Monstropolis area to the park near the current Monsters Inc. ride. The Muppets show would be removed for a roller coaster that will be discussed later. The roller coaster would be the only additional attraction that is known as the plan come after the Mosnters Inc. ride was already in place.

This could have been scrapped because of the high number of Pixar areas such as the Flick's Fun Fair and Cars Land.

Perhaps someday Monsters Inc. will get that coaster made.

Tokyo DisneySea

There are a few reasons that Tokyo DisneySea has so few unplanned rides. The first is that there is little room for expansion in the area as it is located in a dense urban location. The second is that it is fairly new. The final reason that the list of lands that were never built for Tokyo DisneySea is so sparse is the park, like Tokyo Disneyland, is not owned by the Disney company; they only lease the rights to the Oriental Land Company. This means Disney does not put as much energy into the park. If the Oriental Land Company wants to expand, they can let Disney know and Disney can then work on projects for them, but Disney does not often put in extra effort to produce ideas for these parks.

Glacier Bay

While Glacier Bay was not meant to be part of

opening day at DisneySea, it was planned to eventually be included even before the park opened. An area was built that would lead to the land. In the Hotel MiraCosta there is a painting of some concept art for the land.

The area was to be a frozen research outpost. A dark ride or a possible boat ride was planned. A skiing-themed ride based on the same system as the RC Racer ride in Hong Kong was planned. There would also have been an E-ticket attraction, too.

The possibility the land would be made existed for quite some time. However, it looks unlikely now as a new land has been announced for the same location. The land will be based around *Frozen*. It is believed that some aspects of the idea are going to be used for the new land. At the very least the idea of a winter-themed land in DisneySea is happening.

Hong Kong Disneyland

Hong Kong Disneyland is unique because it is a new park with a short history, but it has seen many ideas for lands for its park that were never built. It seems to fly in the face of convention why a small park with such limited space that has been around for such a short time would have so many lands planned but never built.

A few reasons exist. The first is that Disney came up with ideas for multiple areas of the park for later expansion. Often the space had numerous projects that were up for the same space. Because of this method of expansion, many ideas were put forward but only the ones that Disney liked best got the green light.

Another problem with Hong Kong Disneyland was that it was not as popular as it had been hoped it would be. This low attendance made Disney less willing to put as much into the park. However, it also meant that Disney was willing to try to do things to get more people into the park. This mix of a need for something to drive more people into the park but a lack of desire to put much in meant that they would put more into ideas before putting effort into an actual land and any lands would have to be done inexpensively.

Finally, the Hong Kong government is a part owner of the park. The government is supposed to help pay for expansion plans and also approve them. This meant that Disney could spend more money on expansions. But problems would later arise with the government which would affect how Disney would manage the park.

Glacier Bay Hong Kong

Plans for Glacier Bay have already been discussed. Besides placing Glacier Bay in Tokyo, it had also been suggested that it could be put into Hong Kong. The same ideas for Tokyo would have been used for Hong Kong. One major difference was that it would be indoors and include falling snow.

When the park opened it was the smallest of them all and it was decided to make lands outside of the park. Toy Story Land, Mystic Point, and Grizzly Peak would become those lands, but Glacier Bay was supposed to be one of them, too. The main reason the park never made it is the local authorities who have a financial stake in the park did not believe that the idea would work with an Asian audience.

The situation caused problems. The Hong Kong government refused to pay for the design cost. Since the government was not doing what it had agreed to do, Disney was not going to spend money on expansions plans. Disney agreed to make two lands specific to Hong Kong to make the government happy and one that would be exclusive to Asia. The Toy Story Land was chosen to be an Asia exclusive because it could be made fast and cheap and take advantage of the third movie that was to be released around the same time as the land's opening. Grizzly Gulch would be similar to Frontierland but just a little different with rides that were based on other rides but slightly different. Mystic Point would also be similar in that it would use a popular ride but with changes to make it unique.

Isla Tortuga

Isla Tortuga was going to be a pirates-themed land. One reason was to get a pirates ride into the park. Another reason was the popularity of the *Pirates* films at the time. The land would have had a version of the Pirates of the Caribbean. It would also feature shops and a restaurant, and a walk-through attraction. It was also to have a log flume dark ride. A pirate-themed Haunted Mansion was also discussed which may be why Mystic Point got the spot instead. Finally, a water show was also in the planning stages.

Some of the ideas discussed in the Pirate park may have been developed for this land. Most likely this was just one of the many lands in contention for the three spots that would get added to the park.

While pirate fans may be disappointed to hear this land was lost, they should not be too sad as this ultimately would lead to the Treasure Cover at Shanghai which is not the same but has many similarities.

Toontown

As at other parks, Toontown was a possible expansion for Hong Kong Dinseyland. Few details exist, but it is expected to be similar to the other Toontown locations already in other Disney parks, but updated. It would have had an audio-animatronic show which the others do not have.

The debacle with Glacier Bay is likely the reason that Toontown never got made. Disney tried to make the Hong Kong government happy with two totally unique lands and one unique to Hong Kong. It is likely that Toontown was replaced by Toy Story Land since they are both animation-related lands.

While it never was built in Hong Kong, some of the ideas for this version of Toontown may have inspired Toon Studios in Paris.

Frontierland

Frontierland was to be much like the other Frontierlands located around the world. Few other details exist. The Hong Kong version would have featured the Haunted Mansion as well as the It's Tough to Be a Bug show.

The likely reason this land never made it has to do with the Glacier Bay fiasco.

The reality, though, was that Grizzly Gulch would just be a name change to a modified Frontierland so the Disney company could placate the Hong Kong government with little extra work or effort after Hong Kong already backed out of fulfilling its contract over Glacier Bay.

Attractions

When I say "attractions" what I am mostly saying is rides. Rides are for the most part everyone's favorite part of the Disney park experience. While attractions can also include things like shows and parades, little is known about shows or parades that were planned but never created. Due to the lower budgets, there also are less likely to be as many parades or shows that did not see the light of day.

Since attractions are much cheaper than entire parks or lands, there are many more of them that are planned. While attractions may have gone unbuilt for the same reasons as some of the park and lands, attractions often have other reasons they never were built. One common problem that keeps attractions from being built is that a movie that a ride is planned for does not do as well as expected to warrant a new ride being built for that film. Another reason is that the technology may not be where it needs to be to do what the Imagineers have planned for an attraction. Sometimes this initial inability to create a ride the way it is envisioned is only a temporary setback and what never was built can help spark the idea for a ride in the future once the technology has caught up with the imagination of the Imagineers.

Some of the attractions that were planned that did not get made have already been discussed earlier as they would have been in parks or lands that were not built. In some cases what information that was previously mentioned in earlier sections about the ride is all that is known. However, some rides we are more fortunate to know more about from concept art, Imagineers, and even rumors. If more information is known about a ride, it is included here.

One of the worst parts of hearing about rides that never got built is that since they are cheaper and faster to build than lands or parks, they are also more likely to make it off the drawing board. So when you find out a favorite Disney property was going to be used for a ride and it never got off the drawing board, it can be disappointing. The good news is that Disney often goes back to its past and looks at what has been thought of before for inspiration, so if a ride does not eventually get made some part of the idea may end up getting into another attraction.

Disneyland

Disneyland has the largest number of attractions of any park that would be planned but never be built. There are a number of reasons why. The first and most obvious is that Disneyland is the oldest of not only all Disney parks but is often considered the oldest theme park. Just having so many years over the other Disney parks allows Disneyland the chance to have had more attractions planned for it.

Another similar reason that you may not have thought of that would also explain why Disneyland has so many rides is that the idea for Disneyland had been floating around the Disney company for a long time before ground was broken. This adds an added element of time to give a greater chance for rides to be thought of.

Disneyland also has limited space. While an idea may be created easily and may be affordable, the land it would take up may be harder to find. This means getting to be a new Disneyland ride may be harder then becoming a new Epcot ride, for example. The age also plays a factor in that as well. While Mr. Lincoln may not pull in large crowds, devout fans would not want to see it go. No ride at Disneyland has a history at the park as long as attractions like Mr. Lincoln or the Grand Canyon Diorama.

Finally, Disneyland was the only park that Walt Disney would ever step foot in. While Disney came up with the idea for other parks, some of which would never be made ,and some of which would eventually be built after his death in some form or another, only Disneyland was ever directly overseen by Walt Disney when it was operating. Walt was a driving force for creativity in the Disney company. He carefully oversaw all his projects and had the final decision on all changes made to his park. A classic example of the loss of direction with the death of Walt is the Haunted Mansion which he was involved in but did not get to oversee its final construction. Without Walt to direct the team of Imagineers working on the mansion, a debate arose about whether it should be funny or scary which led to a ride which had bits of both but was not completely one or the other. While many great ideas would come after Walt died, the company would face a period when it did not have the direction it once had.

The Disney company would have a later renaissance and have other strong leaders that would help it survive and thrive, but few would deny that Walt Disney was the driving force for the greatest changes and advances at the company. Had Walt Disney lived to see the Magic Kingdom or Epcot finished, they would likely have seen many more rides influenced by him and may have become different parks then they are.

Not all the attractions at Disneyland were thought of when Walt was alive. Even after Walt was gone the Disney Imagineers would come up with other wonderful and not so wonderful ideas for rides that would never get made. While many of these ideas may be lost, we are fortunate to at least know something about the following attractions.

Donald Duck Bumps

Donald Duck Bumps was a very simple ride: bumper boats. However, it did not have much of a chance getting made. In one of two known pieces of concept art featuring the Duck Bumps, they do feature prominently but with two other rides in the same artwork. The other two rides that can be seen include a partial small view of the Dumbo ride and a more prominent view of the Old Mill ride which will soon be talked about. The Duck Bumps at least had a ticket booth already designed featuring Donald Duck in a bumper boat on top with the words Duck Bumps.

Reasons that this ride never was built include a lack of space in Fantasyland where it is believed the ride was planned to be built. The other problem was not enough money when Disneyland was first built to build everything. The Duck Bumps were nothing special and did not really deserve the money being spent on something that could be found at other amusement parks.

While Disneyland would not have any bumper boats, they would see other boat rides such as the short-lived phantom boats and the motor boat cruise ride which was located in Fantasyland like the Duck Bumps would have been. Boats such as water sprites could be rented for a time at the Disneyland Hotel and can be rented at Disney World. Donald would also get his own boat in Toontwon.

The Old Mill

The other ride that would feature in both of the concept art pieces to feature the Duck Bumps was the Old Mill based on the Disney animated short *The Old Mill*. It was planned to be a Ferris wheel. The Duck Bumps are identical in the two concept art pieces that feature the Old Mill with the Duck Bumps, but the Old Mill varies in both design and placement in the two pieces.

The same reasons that the Duck Bumps did not make it apply to the Old Mill. An additional reason is that Walt Disney did not want a Ferris wheel in his park as he connected it to the seedy amusement parks of the day.

While the Old Mill would make it to Disneyland in Anaheim, it would end up getting made in Disneyland Paris. While not exactly the same, they are close. In fact, it really almost does not belong in a list of unbuilt rides since it is pretty much the same, but if I was going to include the Duck Bumps I had to include the Old Mill.

Monstro Shoot-the-Chutes

The Monstro Shoot-the-Chutes was actually planned before Disneyland. A rare piece of concept art shows a version of it planned for the Burbank Mickey Mouse Park. This idea must have been very popular as it would later get two entirely new pieces of concept art which are both more often seen then the first. The ride itself would have been a simple shoot-the-chutes ride but the chute would have been Monstro.

The typical problems that ended so many other rides planned for the park in its opening year would be the undoing of Monstro and his Shoot-the-chutes ride. A lack of funds was the main culprit. Lack of room would be another. It is also possible that it was too similar to other attractions that could be found in amusement parks of the era. It also may have been deemed too scary for children as some ideas for other rides like an initial plan for Mr. Toad were also determined by Walt to not be family friendly because of the thrills.

While the Monstro Shoot-the-chutes would never get made, Monstro would feature in two attractions. Monstro would first appear at the beginning of the Storybook Land Canal Boats. This would be the closest to the version of a full-sized Monstro. Eventually he would appear in the Pinocchio ride in a smaller scale, but he would be used to give a minor scare like he would have as a shoot-the-chutes ride. While a shoot-the-chutes never was made, California Adventure would not only bring back the idea for such a ride but the Grizzly River Rapids would have a drop that would be similar. In the same vein Pirates of the Caribbean would feature a boat drop as would Splash Mountain. So maybe we don't need a simple shoot-the-chutes since we have rides that give us the same experience.

UFO Ride

Little is known about this ride. In the background of one of the earliest park souvenir books you can see concept art for what appears to be a flying saucer ride similar to the rocket jets. Most likely this would be located in Tomorrowland. It was probably not made because the Rocket Jets were made instead.

Peter Pan Crocodile Aquarium

The Peter Pan Crocodile Aquarium was about what it sounds like. It would have been an aquarium that on the outside would have appeared to be a large version of the crocodile from *Peter Pan*. Guests would enter the crocodile through his large gaping mouth and go down into his belly. Once inside the belly, guests would be able to see underwater in a large aquarium full of exotic fish and aquatic life.

The likely reason this was never built was not enough money to build everything when the park was opening, little space, and little reason to build something that was not special for this new park.

While the crocodile never got his own aquarium at Disneyland, eventually Disney would bring back the aquarium on a much larger scale with the Seas Pavilion at Epcot. The Disneyland Hotel for a time had a Peter Pan-themed pool which included a fiberglass crocodile as well, but that has since been replaced with a retro Disneyland park and monorail theme.

Dragon Train

The Dragon Train was probably one of the early designs for the park before Disneyland first opened. It would take guests up and down rolling hills. The head of the dragon appears to be able to move and the dragon would also have breathed smoke rings. Guests would sit inside the dragon's body.

It is possible this would have been where the Casey Jr Circus Train is today, in which case it is likely that Casey Jr fit Disney better then a generic dragon.

It it is possible the Dragon Train may have been the original idea for Casey Jr. The Dragon Train also appears to have made another appearance, as the head of the dragon shown in concept art looks a lot like the sea serpent that would be seen in the Submarine Voyage. Later, the WestCOT plan would also feature a much more aggressive dragon coaster.

Snail Ride

Little is known about this ride. One piece of art shows it from multiple angles including with the bubble top up to see how guests would have been loaded into the snail. What we can see is that it would have been a vehicle in the shape of a snail. I would guess this was planned to be placed somewhere in Fatansyland, but it is hard to say for sure.

Why this was never made is unknown since it is unclear what this was going to be made for or where it would go. It is likely that it was just an idea that didn't have any particular ride in mind, just a design for a possible whimsical vehicle.

While no snail rides or rides with snail vehicles have made it into the Disney parks, the overall look does seem similar to some of the Main Street Electrical Parade floats, so it is possible that someone saw this and was inspired or even made it once long ago and used it for something later.

Fish Boat

The Fish Boat was going to be a boat in the shape of a fish. The only concept art that is known shows the boat from multiple angles and also shows a bubble top and how it would open to allow guest to enter and exit the fish. It is unclear where this would go. The best guess would be that it was for Fantasyland.

This probably never was made because there was not enough money to make it while the park was first being built which is when it is presumed the art was drawn.

While the fish boat never made it into any Disney parks, it is possible that it may have been planned for where the Motor Boat Cruise would go so it may have been a more whimsical take on that. It is possible that a couple years later Disney would finally have the money to put in some boats in that area but maybe not the money to make such elaborate and whimsical boats, or they just preferred more traditional ones.

Uranium Mine

The Uranium Mine was to have guests outside scan for uranium in Tomorrowland. Guests would be given Geiger counters so that they could try to find the hidden uranium in an outdoors desert scene.

I wish I knew why this never was made. Cost was probably one of the reasons. Tomorrowland may have got its name because they figured they would finish the land tomorrow. It was the last land to be finished and they were running out of time and money when they did, which explains why anyone could get a sponsored attraction and most were about what you would expect from a company-sponsored fair exhibit.

This is one idea that will probably not be dug up and used later.

Coffee Made by the Sunday

This is possibly the most accurate and forward thinking of all Tomorrowland exhibits. Not only did they foresee sustainability being popular in the future, they also saw the creation of Starbucks. It appears the idea was this would be a kiosk for coffee but the coffee would be heated or maybe the beans would be roasted by solar cooking.

Possible reasons this never made it off the drawing board include the long time it takes to make a hot cup of coffee relying on the sun and the limited hours of operation for days there is no sun. The overall lack of funds for Tomorrowland also probably played a role in this attraction never seeing the light of day.

Disney would get Starbucks, but beyond that it does not seem that anything even close to this concept ever made it.

Meteorite

This was another exhibit planned for Tomorrowland. It would have been a meteorite on a cement slab. Yes, they were really stretching for things when they were building Tomorrowland. Remember, this is the land that opened with the Hall of Aluminum Fame, would have the Bathroom of Tomorrow, and the Dutch Boy Paint Gallery as exhibits just one year later. The best part of the meteorite is that it would have a black light on it at night which we can assume means it would be some kind of rock that would glow.

Rocks would feature in other Disney attractions such as Nature's Wonderland with its spinning rocks, and Tom Sawyer Island would have a few rocks that guests could play on like the balancing rock. There are various rocks on display throughout the park such as the Yeti footprint in front of the Matterhorn, dinosaur fossils around DinoLand USA, and there may even be a meteorite somewhere in the Mission:SPACE queue, but no rocks have their own exhibit.

Western Union Intrafax Exhibit

The Western Union Intrafax Exhibit was planned for Tomorrowland. The exhibit would be indoors. It is unclear exactly what was planned. Did you see the mechanics of a fax machine? The idea was pretty ahead of its time, but that may have been part of the problem. What could you do with a fax machine in the 1950s?

As it was going to be the Western Union Intrafax Exhibit, it is likely the reason it never was made is that Disney could not get Western Union as a sponsor. They may have had some interest which is why the concept art was made, but they may not have been happy with the cost. While many ideas, even some of the wackier ones, often come back over time, this is not an idea that is likely to ever make it into a park.

Rock Candy Mountain and Rainbow Road to Oz

Rock Candy Mountain was going to look like what it sounds like, a giant mountain made of candy. The mountain would be located where the Storybook Land Canal Boats are. The ride would have Casey Jr go around the mountain. The Storybook Land Canal Boats would go inside the mountain where scenes from the *Wizard of Oz* franchise would be seen as Disney had just bought the rights. The finale would feature a birthday party for Dorothy. This would have changed the ride into the Rainbow Road to Oz.

The ride was originally going to appear to be crystal-like rock candy. Walt Disney decided that it would be impossible to keep the mountain clean with the daily smog in the area and decided the Rock Candy Mountain should be made out of various kinds of candies instead. Concept art was made for the ride as well as various models including models of a number of characters for the Oz scenes.

It was the model of the Rock Candy Mountain itself that would ruin any chance of the ride being built. The Imagineers decided to build a model out of real candy before they realized what a bad idea it would be. The Imagineers felt like it looked like too much candy. What really sealed the Rock Candy Mountain fate was that the room in which they were working on the model did not have air conditioning. The model melted into a huge ugly mess and birds kept coming in and taking bites out of the ride. It was at that point that it was decided the ride would be scrapped.

One thing that could be said to have made it into other Disney attractions was the Winnie the Pooh ride ending with Pooh's birthday just as the Rock Candy Mountain would have ended with Dorothy's.

Adventures in Science

The Adventures in Science ride would have been in Tomorrowland. The ride would have taken guests through a microscope as they traveled through various events in the history of science.

The ride did not get made as planned but would evolve into a ride that was made.

Ultimately, Adventures in Science became Adventures Through Inner Space and focused on science at the molecular level over the history of science.

Cowboy TV

Little is know of this attraction. The only known concept art shows a kid on a fake horse with a western backdrop playing. It is likely that the idea was to film the child in a scene from a western. It is probable that this was planned for Frontierland.

Time and money sent this ride to the glue factory.

Hurricane

The concept for the Hurricane ride is that you would experience going through a hurricane. The ride would place riders in overhead spherical buckets. To simulate the experience it appears they planned to make the ride a dark ride. The ride would have been a mix of Peter Pan and the Skyway.

The most likely reason it never made it was that using the technology they were planning to use might not have given a realistic experience. It is also possible that the ride may have been too expensive to build.

While the Hurricane as originally planned as a dark ride never made it into any of the Disney parks, the idea of a ride through a hurricane would make it into the park. It is likely that the StormRider simulator at Tokyo DisneySea was inspired by Hurricane. With modern technology, the Imagineers finally had a way for guests to experience riding through a hurricane.

Pirates Wax Museum

One of the most famous attractions that would never be built at Disneyland was the Pirates Wax Museum.

The museum was to be located in New Orleans Square. It would have guests walk into a basement to put them outside of the berm and walk through a town with various vignettes of pirates. The pirates would be made of wax like you would see at Madame Tussauds. Many sketches for the Pirates Wax Museum were drawn by Imagineer Marc Davis for the attraction. The ride would feature actual famous pirates, not just nameless ones. However, it was decided that due to the dark nature of real pirates that they would have to make their own less despicable versions.

The Pirates Wax Museum was put on hold during work on the New York World's Fair projects. After the Fair, Imagineering technology had advanced to such a level that a Pirates Wax Museum was no longer cutting edge. Audio-animatronics were made for the Fair that raised the bar on any new Disney rides.

The simplicity of a Pirates Wax Museum was not the only reason it was canceled. Along with audio-animatronics, the New York World's Fair also brought new methods of moving guests through. These new methods allowed for much greater ride capacity letting more guests go through an attraction per hour. While getting more guests through per hour is very important now, at that time guests paid for each ride so it was even more important to get as many people though a ride per hour as possible. A walk-through attraction would not be able to move as many people as the new ride systems developed for the fair could.

This ended up being a positive story as the Pirates Wax Museum actually got an upgrade, evolving into the Pirates of the Caribbean. That ride would become one of the most popular Disney rides and is considered by many to be one of the best dark rides of all time. The ride would even lead to the successful movie franchise of the same name. The movie franchise would then influence updates to the ride and even affect later Disney attractions. Disneyland Shanghai would go on to receive its own pirate-themed land, Treasure Cove.

Museum of the Weird

The Museum of the Weird is one of the most well-known parts of Disney history that never came to life. The reason that the Museum of the Weird is so famous is that various concept work for the Museum of the Weird was shown on TV with Imagineer Rolly Crump talking about it with Walt Disney and showing his work for the project. It was never fully decided where or how to incorporate the museum. When Walt first saw the work he stayed up all night trying to think of a way to incorporate the Museum of the Weird into the Haunted Mansion. It was Walt not Rolly Crump who came up with the idea of using it at either the beginning or the end of the attraction, and even the name itself.

The Museum of the Weird would feature many odd things. As its name suggests, it is hard to put into words what it was exactly. There would be a chair that could move and talk, a melting candle man, mushroom people, a Gypsy cart, and many other unusual things collected from around the world.

At first no one liked the idea until Walt saw it and showed great interest. Once Walt died, though, the Haunted Mansion lost direction. The mansion had two competing camps. One group of Imagineers wanted a scary ride. The other group wanted a funny ride. In the past when creative differences arose Walt Disney would decide. Not only was Walt the boss but his opinion and understanding of what would work with guests was respected by the Imagineers. Ultimately, the idea for the Museum of the Weird was scrapped during this time and became a lost soul of an idea.

While the Museum of the Weird never was its own part of the Haunted Mansion, it would come back from the dead over the years. The Haunted Mansion would borrow a little from the museum with the wall paper having a similar design to some of the concept art for the Museum of the Weird and the talking chair became the chair which many think has Donald's face on it. Besides those few parts that would make it into the mansion, the Magic Kingdom would use the Gypsy cart to sell merchandise. A Disney comic, *Seekers of the Weird*, would be inspired by it. Finally, during a recent refurbishment of Thunder Mountain in Orlando, a letter in the queue would reference the Museum of the Weird.

Herbie the Love Bug

After the second *Herbie* film, Disney thought about making a Herbie ride. The ride would have been very ambitious and based on the concept art it appears it would have been an outside attraction.

Much like Rocket Rods, Herbie would speed up and rear up as he takes off at the start of the ride. Next Herbie would be in a chicken race and just miss the other car. Following the near miss you would ride on two wheels while on the edge of a cliff. Then Herbie would zigzag through a line up of cars in town leading to the start of a Tijuana Road race which would see you go under a car being towed. You would then go through a "shack" followed shortly by splitting the whole vehicle in half to avoid a cactus. How the car would split is unclear as one concept art piece shows it splitting like in the movie down the middle with a right half and a back half. Another concept piece shows a family in the vehicle as it splits in half front to back.

After coming back together we find ourselves in San Francisco. In San Francisco we would have many more hair-raising adventures such as leaping over buildings, nearly missing a trolley car, and even riding up the Golden Gate bridge just like in the *Herbie* movies.

After leaving San Francisco, we would go through a mine shaft and narrowly miss some mine carts. To end the ride, Herbie would skip across the water.

As plans for the ride were supposedly made after the second film and with two more major motion pictures planned in the near future, popularity does not seem to be the reason this ride never was built. Two factors are the likely cause of its failure to be made.

The first problem is size. While I have heard Fantasyland was the planned location with such a large area and the caves and desert scenes, I think it is possible that the Nature's Wonderland area may have been a better fit. But anywhere they put the ride, even if it was made into a dark ride, it would require lots of space which is at a premium at Disneyland.

The last reason is most likely the biggest reason of all. It was just too far ahead of its time. Even just the first gimmick of rearing up would prove difficult decades later with the Rocket Rods. Most of the crazy stunts Herbie would have to pull would be hard to do at all, but trying to do all of them with the same single vehicle seems like an impossible feat, even for Herbie.

While the ride was never built, a Herbie parade did make it into Disneyland. A parade may not be much compared to what may have been an E-ticket attraction, but at least it shows Disney loves the love bug.

Garden of the Gods

The Garden of the Gods was to be a replacement for the Storybook Land Canal Boats. Guests would sit in a horse chariot vehicle. The vehicle would ride along an aqueduct across various fountains. One scene would have you go by a snowy village. The real excitement came when you got to Hades. You would see fire-breathing faces in what is likely the river Styx with Cerberus guarding the entrance. Then you would go inside and see Hades himself.

It is unclear why this ride was never built. It is possible the idea of going to hell may have been too scary although not far from the same spot you would do the same thing at Mr. Toad's. It may have been too expensive to make the change. There may not have been enough room for the whole project in the small space it was being planned for. Or people may have preferred what was already there.

This may not sound like a ride that really got into other parts of the Disney empire, but the concept art for the snow village does look similar to the Peter and the Wolf scene in the Disneyland Paris Storybook Land Canal Boats.

Space Voyage

The idea for Space Voyage came after the success of the Matterhorn. Space Voyage would have been a more ambitious version of Space Mountain featuring four separate tracks.

The idea never made it because there was not enough land. Money may also have been a factor.

While the Space Voyage never was built, it would lead to the creation of Space Mountain. Space Mountain would not feature as many tracks, but the general premise would be the same.

Fantasia Gardens

Fantasia Gardens was a planned overlay for the Motor Boat Cruise which had nothing to see and had experienced lower and lower attendance. The ride would add in statues, music, and water features.

The reason the ride did not get the overlay is that the nearby Autopia made too much noise and the whole experience would not be pleasant.

While the Motor Boat Cruise did not get a Fantasia overlay, it would also get a short-term Gummi Bears overlay before sailing into the sunset.

The Enchanted Snow Palace

The Enchanted Snow Palace was going to be housed in a glacier building. The ride was the brain child of Marc Davis and was based on the idea that it would provide a place to cool off from the warm California sun. The ride would be a boat ride through a magical northern world with playful polar bears, penguins, walruses, and elves. Toward the end of the ride you would get to see the beautiful Snow Queen herself.

The concept art gives us a glimpse of a cute, beautiful ride but not one that is very thrilling. At the time Disney was looking to find thrilling and exciting new rides. The Enchanted Snow Palace may have been a piece of dark ride art in the era of It's a Small World, but in a later era it was too tame for park executives.

The ride may have influenced the movie *Frozen* and even the Frozen ride.

Fireworks Factory

The Fireworks Factory was planned to be part of Discovery Bay. The ride would be similar to the Buzz Lightyear ride in that guests would be shooting and interacting with the ride. It would take place in a fireworks factory and you would shoot various fireworks targets with hits creating effects.

The obvious reason this ride never made it was that Discovery Bay never made it. While the Fireworks Factory ride never made it into Disneyland, a Fireworks Factory did make it into Toontown which had been inspired by this ride.

The Black Hole

The Black Hole ride was going to replacing the aging Adventures Through Inner Space. The movie of the same name was an attempt by Disney to get into the science-fiction genre which was popular with youth at the time. The ride was an extension of that. The Black Hole was going to be a simulator ride based on the movie. It would be cutting edge at the time. Not only would it be a thrilling simulator adventure, it was going to allow you to choose your own path as well.

There were two main causes for the Black Hole ride being sucked into the void. The first and most obvious reason was that *The Black Hole* did not do as well at the box office as Disney had hoped. The second problem was the cost of the ride. It would have cost more then twice the film's budget.

You should be able to figure out what ride was influenced by the Black Hole: Star Tours. The one thing that the Black Hole had in its favor though was being able to choose what you did. Many years later Star Tours would give you multiple locations to go, but they would be out of your control. The Epcot ride Horizons would feature three endings and allowed guests to vote on which ending they wanted to see. So the Black Hole not only led to the popular Star Tours, ride it also may have had some influence on the lost Horizons ride.

The Black Hole Part II

Disney really believed in *The Black Hole*. Their other idea was to have a dark ride shooter. The ride would have you shoot at targets while you rode through space in a traditional dark ride.

Much like the grander simulator ride, it was the box office that sucked this idea back into the darkness. It is possible that the simulator would have been built if *The Black Hole*, and this was their backup if it did not.

Much like the other Black Hole ride idea that did not make it, this idea would be mined for inspiration when the Imagineers were creating Buzz Lightyear Space Ranger Spin.

Tron

Tron had a similar history to *The Black Hole*. Disney once more had high hopes for this film. Before it was out, they revamped the Black Hole shooter dark ride to a *Tron* theme. The ride would have replaced another aging Tomorrowland attraction, Mission to Mars.

The reason Tron was deleted was that the film did not make enough money at the box office.

The dark ride shooter as you all know would eventually make it to become Buzz Lightyear Space Ranget Spin and even Toy Story Mania. The Tron light tunnel would end up as part of the PeopleMover. Finally, Shanghai Disneyland would get its own Tron Lightcycle ride.

The Black Cauldron

The Black Cauldron would have a similar history as *Tron* and *The Black Hole*. Disney again was hoping to have some box office magic with *The Black Cauldron*. Not much is known about the ride, with very little concept art existing. What is known is that it was to be a dark ride using a boat.

Much like the last few entries on this list, *The Black Cauldron* would not meet box office hopes for Disney. In fact, it lost money for the studio. Disney viewed *The Black Cauldron* as a failure and wanted to separate itself from the film for some time. It was not until it started to get a cult following that Disney has started to embrace it.

With such poor box office performance, a Black Cauldron attraction may seem unlikely but the end segment of the Cinderella Castle Mystery Tour featured a child participant vanquishing the horned king. Not only would the Tokyo Disneyland Cinderella Castle Mystery Tour be influenced by the ride that never was, but magically another ride would be influenced by it as well. The boats shown in the concept art greatly resemble the boats used in the Maelstrom ride.

Alternative Michael Jackson Films

Disney came up with three ideas for a 3D Michael Jackson film. Disney wanted three story ideas in just three days. The first idea was to have Michael Jackson as a mythical figure in a medieval forest fairy-tale setting. The Ice Queen was going to be the villain and it was Michael Jackson who would melt her heart. The other rejected concept was to have Michael Jackson in the park after hours. While in the park the audio animatronics would come to life and dance with him.

When the three ideas were put in front of Michael Eisner and Frank Wells, they choose what was to become *Captain EO*. Then George Lucas and Michael Jackson also picked the story that would become *Captain EO*. With the *Captain EO* story the unanimous winner, the other ideas were long forgotten.

If the Ice Queen story was written first, then it probably inspired the *Captain EO* story as it is very similar. It is unlikely that these ideas will inspire any more Disney attractions.

Circus Hot Air Balloons

The Circus Hot Air Balloons would have transported guests from Discovery Bay to Dumbo's Circus Land like the Skyway transported guests from Fantasyland to Tomorrowland. The ride would have been made to look like hot air balloons.

The obvious reason this ride was never built is because neither of the lands it would have sent people to ever were built. Even if they had made either land it is possible that with a very similar ride already operating nearby, they may not have made this ride anyway.

With the demise of the Skyway around the Disney parks of the world, it is unlikely that a hot air balloon version will ever be brought back.

Circus Disney

Circus Disney was going to be one of the main attractions of Dumbo's Circusland. The ride would be a dark ride featuring animatronics of a wide variety of popular and less well-known Disney characters. Many miniature pieces were made featuring characters such as a fire-breathing Reluctant Dragon and a one-man-band Horace Horsecollar. There would also be circus animals featuring favorites from *The Jungle Book* as well as less popular characters such as some of the animated characters from *Bedknobs and Broomsticks*. Finally, guests would go inside the big top itself and see Dumbo and a daredevil Goofy.

The obvious reason this ride never was built is that the land which it was going to be placed in was never built. It is a shame as some well-loved but lesser-known characters would have had a chance to make it into a ride.

The concept greatly influenced the look and feel of the Magic Kingdom's Storybook Circus.

Mickey's Madhouse

Mickey's Madhouse was another dark ride planned for Dumbo's Circusland. This ride, though, would have Mickey Mouse as the main character. The ride would focus on Mickey in his early black-and-white years. As the name suggests, it was going to be a bit crazy. The ride was going to be a mix of dark ride and roller coaster. The ride would have had a story to it unlike many other roller coasters such as Space Mountain which are just there.

As you probably can guess, the reason this ride never made it to the real world was that the Dumbo's Circusland idea never really flew off.

Nautilus Walk Through

A walk-through attraction of the *Nautilus* was planned for Discovery Bay. A *Nautilus* sub would be parked in the bay and you would walk down into it and even get to see scenes from the movie. There would also be a restaurant in the *Nautilus*.

The reason this didn't get made was that Discovery Bay area was never made.

This may not have made it into Disneyland, but the *Nautilus* would get docked in both DisneySea as well as Disneyland Paris. In Paris, the concept of a walk-through *Nautilus* attraction would see fulfillment.

Captain Nemo's Adventure

Captain Nemo's Adventure was another attraction planned for Discovery Bay. It would have been a simulator ride. The ride would have started with an audio-animatronic preshow featuring Captain Nemo. The theater would have been huge with over 100 guests. We would go undersea to see gardens, Nemo's men, sunken ships, glowing fish, and finally a giant squid. The giant squid would not only be seen outside the sub but an animatronic tentacle would open the hatch at one point and get in. Finally, we would arrive at the surface safe and sound.

Yet again we have an attraction that was never built because the Discovery Bay area was never built, although it is possible the technology of the time may have kept it from being fully realized. Later, Star Tours would hold less then half the same number of guests.

Eventually, a use for simulator technology would be found for Star Tours and a few other Disney rides.

Professor Marvel's Gallery of Wonders

Professor Marvel's Gallery of Wonders was to be a show set in a revolving building much like Carousel of Progress. The show would feature Professor Marvel who would show you both his strange collection of animals as well as some of his fantastic experiments. Along the way we would be introduced to his purple pet dragon.

This was again lost to us because the Discovery Bay project never was built.

Tony Baxter was involved in this project and you may also know he was involved in another project later for Epcot. Professor Marvel would end up as the Dreamfinder and his purple pet dragon would end up as Figment. The Journey into Imagination ride was inspired by concepts for Professor Marvel's Gallery of Wonders. While Professor Marvel's Gallery of Wonders may not have been made as planned, it did end up being the seed of an idea for the much-loved Journey into Imagination ride.

Western Balloon Ascent

The Western Balloon Ascent would have been the other side of the already mentioned Circus Hot Air Balloon. If you got on in Circusland it would be known as the Circus Hot Air Balloons but from Discovery Bay it was known as the Western Balloon Ascent.

While this attraction also failed to rise from the drawing table because Discovery Bay was never built, it also would have required Dumbo's Circusland to be built as well. So this time Discovery Bay is only partially responsible.

Like Circus Hot Air Balloon, ride this ride is unlikely to make a comeback with a closure of all similar rides at the various parks around the world.

The Island at the Top of the World

The Island at the Top of the World would take guests on a trip on the airship *Hyperion*. The ride would have been a dark ride similar to Peter Pan in that it would be overhead. The ride would mix various technologies such as miniatures and projections. Riders would start out going to the North Pole and see an aurora borealis and native Nordic creatures. Things get a bit more magical as you head into an ice maze. Eventually, you enter Astragard which is full of exotic beasts. A storm takes you away from the amazing scenes that unfold and you are forced to turn back.

The movie *The Island at the Top of the World* did not do well and is the reason the ride and the land were never built. Discovery Bay probably could have survived on its own had Disney wanted to go ahead, but with the failure of the *The Island at the Top of the World* movie the The Island at the Top of the World ride would not make it.

The Island at the Top of the World ride never made it, but the concept art for the hangar would be the inspiration for the hangar and *Hyperion* at Disneyland Paris' Discoveryland.

The Spark Gap Coaster

The Spark Gap Coaster was to be a small family coaster. The ride would have featured Tesla coils that would shoot out sparks of electricity. It would have been part of the second phase expansion of Discovery Bay.

Since Discovery Bay never made it in the first place, all second phase rides never made it too.

So far, no one has been turned on by the concept for this ride.

The Tower

The Tower was another Discovery Bay second-phase expansion ride. Less is known about this ride than the others. It would have used electromagnets for propulsion. The Tower would have been another roller coaster. It would have likely been the more adult counterpart to the Spark Gap Coaster.

Without a Discovery Bay there would be no Discovery Bay rides, including the Tower.

Disney has started using electromagnets in some of their roller coasters such as California Screamin' and Rock 'n' Roller Coaster. This may have been where the first ideas for the use of magnets for accelerated propulsion came from.

The Voyage Thru Time/Lost World/Lost River Rapids.

One idea that had many names and many versions was Voyage Thru Time/Lost World/ Lost River Rapids. The ride would be a boat attraction of some kind. In one version it was similar to a modern rapids ride. The ride was being planned both as an indoor and an outdoor attraction with the possibility of having both indoor and outdoor segments. The ride would have featured a trip that would take you through a land of dinosaurs. Not only does concept art exist but a model for Discovery Bay also features dinosaurs in the river, leading one to believe that it was part of the ride.

The rides would have been part of the second phase of Discovery Bay. With no Discovery Bay it was another ride that would become extinct.

It is possible that it may have inspired DINOSAUR at Disney's Animal Kingdom to some degree. Also the idea to have a rapids ride did end up in multiple Disney parks around the world but without the dinosaurs.

Indiana Jones and the Lost Expedition

The Indiana Jones and the Lost Expedition was part of a much larger plan for the Indiana Jones ride. The Indiana Jones and the Lost Expedition would have featured the ride we have now, but it would also see changes to the Jungle Cruise as well as an additional mine car roller coaster. The Jungle Cruise ride would be rerouted to the Indiana Jones and the Lost Expedition complex as well as go through the complex.

At the time the Indiana Jones and the Lost Expedition was being proposed, another idea was also being put forward. Splash Mountain was the other idea. Splash Mountain had some advantages. The first was that it would be cheaper since it was just one ride and it could reuse the America Sings audio-animatronics. Splash Mountain would also give the park a water ride as well as a second attraction in the small Critter Country. Ultimately, Splash Mountain won out because it not only was cheaper but also could bring some things that were needed to the park such as a water ride.

The entire Indiana Jones and the Lost Expedition was not lost, however. Eventually, the Indiana Jones ride was built in Disneyland. Even the mine car roller coaster made it into Disneyland Paris. It never got its own mini-land or Jungle Cruise refurbishment, but most of the ideas made it into the parks.

The Great Movie Ride

The Great Movie Ride was a possible addition that was planned to be added to Disneyland. The ride would have been a clone of the one in Orlando. It would have been located in Hollywoodland.

Since Hollywoodland never got green-lit, the Great Movie Ride never did either.

For now, there is only one Great Movie Ride.

Dick Tracy's Crime Stoppers

Dick Tracy's Crime Stoppers was going to be an E-ticket attraction for the Hollywoodland area of the park. It was also planned for Orlando. The ride would be the first shooting ride and also the first ride to use the system that Indiana Jones would use. You would be in a car that would give you a unique experience each time and you would also be able to shoot at targets. The ride would be based around the *Dick Tracy* film.

The ride was never built for a number of reasons. The first reason it was never built is that Hollywoodland was never built. However, it could have been built in Florida still. Another reason it was not built was that unlike Buzz Lightyear where you are shooting aliens, Dick Tracy's Crime Stoppers would have you shooting at "real" people. Finally, the *Dick Tracy* film did not perform as well as expected. There had been plans to make a sequel to *Dick Tracy*, but legal problems mixed with a lower-than-expected return at the box office for the first film meant Dick Tracy's Crime Stoppers was dead on arrival.

The ride vehicle's platform would make it into the Indiana Jones ride and the target shooting aspect would also make it into Buzz Lightyear's Space Ranger Spin.

Superstar Television

Superstar Television would have been in Hollywoodland. It would have allowed guests to act out famous scenes from TV shows.

The show never happened since Hollywoodland never happened.

It was inspired from pre-existing shows in Orlando, though it would have been different from such shows had it been made.

Geyser Mountain

Geyser Mountain was going to be located in Frontierland to give it an additional thrill. It would have used the Tower of Terror ride system but changed the story to be that you were riding a drilling machine when you get caught by a geyser going off and you get thrown high into the air with the geyser. The concept went pretty far as architectural drawings were made for the attraction and models. The ride would feature more ride elements including some scenes reminiscent of the old mine train ride and a section across a rickety old bridge. The ride also would have been sent to Disneyland Paris.

By now it should be obvious why the Disneyland Paris version never made it. Even though it was estimated it would cost much less then Tower of Terror as it would not require the same research-and-development budget, it was still considered too expensive a project at the time.

No Geyser Mountain ever went off at a Disney park, but Disneyland and Disneyland Paris would ultimately both receive a copy of the original Twilight Zone Tower of Terror.

Lightkeepers

Lightkeepers was going to be a parade that would debut with the New Tomorrowland. The Lightkeepers parade would have replaced the Main Street Electrical parade which was seen as being outdated at the time. It would utilize state-of-the-art music and lighting technology.

The idea for the parade was based around aliens coming to Disneyland. Fortunately, they are nice aliens. The aliens were known as Lightkeepers which is where the parade gets its name. The parade would start with a UFO landing backstage for all to see and hear. Then the Lightkeepers would come out glowing from within. Then a light-and-sound extravaganza would take place.

The main reason that the Lightkeepers parade never landed in the park was that the cost was too high during the Disneyland Paris fiasco.

Disney still wanted to replace the dated Main Street Electrical Parade but did not want to spend as much. So instead they came up with the Light Magic Parade which ended up being a sore spot for Disney as it ended up being a costly disappointment that Disney rarely brings up.

ExtraTERRORrestrial Alien Encounter

ExtraTERRORrestrial Alien Encounter was going to land at Disneyland. In fact, it was originally going to land at Disneyland before it landed in the Magic Kingdom. The ride was part of the Tomorrowland 2055 plan. It would have been placed in the former Mission to Mars theater.

ExtraTERRORrestrial Alien Encounter was finished in Orlando before it could be finished at Disneyland. While it was still planned that Disneyland would get the ride, the Tomorrowland 2055 plan ended up not materializing and neither would ExtraTERRORrestrial Alien Encounter at Disneyland.

The ride did make it to the Magic Kingdom.

Plectu's Intergalactic Revue

Plectu's Intergalactic Revue also went by a variety of other names including P.T. Quantum's Fantastic Galactic Showboat Extraordinaire. The idea was to have an audio-anaimatronic show with aliens in the Carousel Theater. The show would have been part of the Tomorrowland 2055 changes. The Imagineers came up many different versions for the show. They all revolved around the general idea of aliens putting on a show of some kind.

While the failure of Tomorrowland 2055 to get off the ground is an obvious reason the show never went on, even had the Tomorrowland 2055 taken flight it is unlikely that any version of the show would have made it. While the Imagineers repeatably tried to sell Michael Eisner on various versions of the show, he was not impressed with the idea. The audio-animatronic shows were not particularly popular and getting to be old as well as being expensive and hard to maintain. So it is unlikely such a show would have been made even if the rest of the project had.

This is unlikely to make it into our world anytime soon.

Young Indiana Jones Stunt Spectacular

The Young Indiana Jones Stunt Spectacular was going to go in the area that the new Star Wars land is now being built. The show came about because of the success of the Indiana Jones Stunt show in Orlando. This time the show would focus on a young Indiana Jones as seen in the TV series. The show would take a different direction than the one in Florida. This time it would be a story not a behind-the-scenes show. The show would feature old Indiana Jones recalling his youth. It would be housed in a circus tent with the Disneyland Railroad running right through the show. The train would actually be a part of the show.

There is no known reason this show never made it. It is possible that it would have been too difficult in many respects such as integrating the Disneyland Railroad into the show.

While the show never made it, a hearse that was made for the show can be seen in front of the Haunted Mansion. An urban rumor exists that it is the hearse that carried Brigham Young but that makes little sense. Besides the hearse in front of the Haunted Mansion, Indiana Jones would make it into multiple Disney parks although work had been ongoing for Indiana Jones to enter the park before the show.

Atlantis Expedition

The Atlantis Expedition was going to be a replacement for the Submarine Voyage. While there was a tent put up with an announcement stating the ride would open in the future, it was not approved by management and only placed by the Imagineers. The ride would have been themed to the *Atlantis: The Lost Empire* animated film. The subs would have had hands that you could use to grab gold and gems you found. Unfortunately, guests would encounter a leviathan which would attack the sub and even cause a leak in the sub. When you finally got back to the surface safely, you would have lost most of your treasure except for a coin for each guest.

For those of you who even recall the movie *Atlantis: The Lost Empire*, you will remember it didn't make much of an impression on most people or the box office. Disney was not going to spend the money on a ride for a movie that did not do well.

Atlantis would not get a ride, but the subs would ultimately return themed to *Finding Nemo*. In DisneySea, while you don't get to control a mechanical hand, you do get to control a flashlight.

Star Tours Podracer

It was felt that Star Tours needed an upgrade. After *Phantom Menace* came out, the best possible ride experience was a pod race. Fortunately, no one decided to switch films to a pod race, but they waited to update Star Tours until there was more to work with.

Star Tours did get an update and it would include the chance for you to be in a pod race, but it would feature many more options, too.

3D Haunted Mansion

Little is known about this concept except for one piece of concept art. It appears that there was some plan for either an update or whole new Haunted Mansion at a new park that would feature a trackless system and be in 3D. With so little information about this possible update, it is hard to say why it never happened.

A trackless system was created for the Hong Kong version of the mansion. It is possible the design may have been for Hong Kong and not an update for other pre-existing versions.

Tron Lightcyles Coaster

According to rumor, the Tron Lightcyles Coaster was supposed to get placed in Tomorrowland where the old PeopleMover went. It was supposed to be similar to the Shanghai Disneyland version.

It is unlikely that the ride would work in the location proposed. The PeopleMover track seems only suited for a PeopleMover. Also, the Shanghai version has indoor elements. *Tron* the film did not do as well as had been hoped but was going to get a sequel. However, Disney has too much on its plate with *Star Wars* and Marvel, so *Tron* took a back seat.

If the Tron Lightcyles Coaster is popular in Shanghai, it is possible it will end up somewhere else in the Disney empire.

Walt Disney World: Magic Kingdom

The Magic Kingdom is the second oldest of the parks which has given it lots of time to see ride ideas come and go. Unlike Disneyland which has limited room, there is plenty of room around the Magic Kingdom which lends itself to new rides being able to be opened.

Western River Expedition

The Western River Expedition is one of the most famous of all lost rides. It made it far into development and even had models built. The ride was designed by Marc Davis and the concept art shows his classic comical bent. The ride was going to be the East Coast version of the Pirates of the Caribbean since Florida was so close to the Caribbean they felt they should do something else, like the Wild West. The ride would have been a boat ride similar to Pirates with guests loading indoors under a night sky. With the low water table guests would go up a waterfall instead of down it as you do in Pirates. Then guests would see some amusing scenes of nature with animals and plants. Guests would see a stagecoach robbery. Then guests would go under the railroad tracks and enter Dry Gulch. The town of Dry Gulch would include some silly scenes of Western life including cowboys, saloon girls, and bank robberies. You would leave the town and see some Native American scenes including a rain dance. You would encounter some bandits but get away by going down a waterfall.

Besides the ride itself there would also be a mine train roller coaster, hiking trails on top of a mesa, a Pueblo village, and a pack mule ride in an area that would be known as Thunder Mesa.

There were two causes for the demise of this attraction. The first was that after the park opened so many people wanted to know where the Pirates were. Disney realized they had been wrong about Florida having had enough of pirates. The second problem was the cost as it would have been the largest show building ever and would have been very expensive to build.

While the Western River Expedition never was built, a mine train would end up at the Magic Kingdom and the other parks.

Nostromo

Nostromo was going to be a dark ride based on the movie *Aliens*. The ride would be placed in Tomorrowland. The ride was yet another one planned to feature a gun. It would have you board the Nostromo like in the movie and shoot aliens with your laser gun.

The reason the ride never made it was because it was so out of this world for Disney. Many at Disney felt it was too scary and not appropriate for a Disney park.

Ultimately, Nostromo would lead to the development of the ExtraTERRORrestrial Alien Encounter.

Besides leading to that attraction, you would eventually get to board the Nostromo and come face to face with the alien from the film in the Great Movie Ride.

Flying Saucers

The Flying Saucers were slated to appear in the Magic Kingdom in Tomorrowland. They would be similar to the earlier Flying Saucers at Disneyland but they would be indoors. The original Flying Saucers had worked great during testing when they were in a controlled environment indoors; there is even a famous picture of Walt riding them during testing. However, once you take it outdoors in an uncontrolled environment it becomes a mess to keep working right. So this time Disney was going to do it right and do it indoors.

The main reason the plan was scrapped is that it was part of a bigger development for Disney that also was scrapped. Money also was a major issue.

For a short time a hover0based ride would come back to the Disney parks as Luigi's Flying Tires. This was also located outside like the former Disneyland Flying Saucers and never worked out well either, so was closed shortly after opening. Hopefully next time the idea comes up they will keep the ride indoors.

Fire Mountain

Two different mountains were planned for the Magic Kingdom. Fire Mountain was one of those mountains. It was decided to be the first one built since it would be cheaper to put it in than the other. Fire Mountain would start out as a traditional roller coaster on rails but once the volcano you were riding around goes off it becomes an overhead roller coaster instead. The ride had originally been planned for Fantasyland but had little to attach it to Fantasyland other than it was to replace the 20,000 Leagues Under the Sea area. So it was moved to Adventureland where it would fit in perfectly. Disney went so far as to send a balloon to the height of the top of the volcano to see if it would protrude on the view from Main Street. The Volcano would not interfere and actually could be seen when viewed from the Polynesian Resort.

Ultimately, it was decided that it would cost to much to build the ride considering that it was going to be a thrill ride in a park that was geared for families. The price tag may have been okay for a more adult-themed park, but it was decided it was not worth the investment for the Magic Kingdom.

A ride through a volcano would appear at DisneySea, and Fire Mountain may have been part of the inspiration for that, but the ride itself is very different.

Bald Mountain/Villain Mountain

Bald Mountain/Villain Mountain were the two names for the other planned ride that Fire Mountain was up against. Bald Mountain had been at times planned to be a log flume ride like Splash Mountain, a roller coaster, or even both in the same mountain. So many ideas were created that it was decided to make it a whole land. Because it would cost more and take more time to create a whole land, Fire Mountain was decided to be built first. The ride would pit riders against famous Disney villains until at the end the riders would barely escape the villains by going down the log flume drop. Little is know about the coaster aspect of the mountain. It is likely that Villain Mountain would have been the final name since few guests knew what Bald Mountain was and many were confused by it, thinking it was a hairless mountain.

A mixture of factors kept the mountain from awakening. The first was the postponement to make way for Fire Mountain. Next, its own success led to further delay as the villain land was considered for a whole new park, not just a land. With all the waiting, things just never came together for the ride, land, or park.

Rumors are always going around about a new park for Disney World. Mostly they are that Disney will create a thrill park geared for older audiences. It is possible that someday an entire villain park, land, or at least ride may make it into the realm of the living.

Monorail Expansion

This is one that keeps coming up over and over. Disney has even made signs showing new monorail stations would be placed soon, but they never have.

Anyone who has been on Disney property knows one of the best ways to get around is the monorail. It is convenient and fast. However, it is also very expensive to add in more track. It is the initial track expense that keeps it from happening.

This is one of those persistent rumors that may happen. The biggest issue would be the economics of adding the rail over time vs other transportation methods.

Matterhorn

Disney World almost had a Matterhorn. The start of the ride would have guests experience a blizzard to allow them to cool down from the hot Florida weather. Besides that, it is expected to be very similar to the Disneyland version.

No reason is known why it was never made.

While the Matterhorn never made it to Disney World, a Yeti did. The Matterhorn idea, though, would continue to be brought up in Florida, as we will see later.

Fantasia Gardens II

Fantasia Gardens was going to replace the Swan Boats. The ride would feature six sections all based on the movie *Fantasia*. The ride would not be too exciting and would feature mostly topiary scenes. At one point, guests would be headed straight into topiary brooms with water coming from buckets headed toward guests which would stop right before hitting them.

A lack of sponsors is the reason this ride never set sail.

Fantasia would continue to inspire other possible rides, as we will see later.

Duck Tales Dark Ride

Little is known about this proposed attraction. It is believed to have been planned for Mickey's Starland. Most of the information about the ride comes from a rare overseas special edition of the *Duck Tales* TV show DVD set. The information is only available as a rare secret Easter egg.

With such little information, it is hard to tell why this ride never was built.

While the ride was never built, Disneyland would have a special Disney Afternoon Avenue which would feature wooden cutouts of *Duck Tales* characters as well as a money bin ball pit.

Meet the Robinsons

A refurbishment of the Tomorrowland Speedway was considered that would be based on *Meet the Robinsons*. The ride would have guests ride spaceships that would be cars held up in the air. It would not be too exciting but something different.

The two probable reasons this did not happen is the cost and the lack of success of the film.

Unless *Meet the Robinsons* gains a cult following, it is unlikely this will get built, although we can always hope that some kind of upgrade for the Speedway happens.

Haunted Mansion Holiday

Disney created an entire second Haunted Mansion Holiday overlay for Walt Disney World. However, the management at the park was not interested in putting it to use.

This was not an issue of a lack of funds, it was a lack of interest. For some reason the project got completed without first finding out it was not wanted.

It ended up being fine, since Disney just sent the whole overlay including all props it had prepared for Disney World to Disneyland Tokyo instead. Tokyo Disneyland would accept the new overlay and use it.

Cinderella Chateau

When the original Fantasyland update was announced it was planned that there would be a Cinderella chateau. Since the castle in the Magic Kingdom is Cinderella's, it would make sense to place such an attraction. The attraction would be both a meet and greet as well as a chance to see the Fairy Godmother making Cinderella's dress. The chateau would have been an interactive experience.

The reason this did not get made is that the whole area was themed for girls and didn't have anything to appeal to boys. So the area that would house the various princesses was replaced with the mine train ride instead. Also, it was decided that they should get as many princesses as they could instead of focusing only on a few. Money may also have played a part as all the interactivity can be expensive and instead they went with a simple, cheap meet and greet.

Briar Rose Cottage

The Briar Rose Cottage was going to be placed near the Cinderella Chateau and been a more humble version in size. The fairies would have added some great interactive fun to the cottage. Fans of Sleeping Beauty would be able to meet her in person.

As mentioned with Cinderella, the area was too focused on little girls. Also, the princesses were limited. So an all inclusive meet and greet was made instead along with the mine train ride to be more family friendly.

Being so recent it is unlikely we will see the plans reused soon, but they may make it into one of the parks in time.

Pixie Hollow

Pixie Hollow was planned to be part of the updated Magic Kingdom Fantasyland. It would feature a meet and greet with the pixies. The area was announced, and concept art and models were made.

Multiple problems ended Pixie Hollow. The first was that the land was focused too much on little girls. The second problem was that the pixies were losing popularity. So the pixies were replaced with the Storybook Circus section of the expansion.

Unless people start liking the pixies again, it is unlikely that this area will ever be built.

Epcot

Epcot, like other Disney World properties, has lots of room. This allows it to have lots of rides and see lots of new rides added. Even though it is not as old as the Magic Kingdom, it has seen a large number of ride ideas that were never built. A good reason for this is that when the park was being built they were trying to get as many countries to come on board with them and sponsor an area. They also wanted them to put in as much as possible. This led to many ideas for rides to be created.

Almost all the rides that have been planned for Epcot but never made it were ones planned for country pavilions, although a few Future World Pavilion rides have been planned that never made it past the drawing board.

Mary Poppins

The Mary Poppins attraction would have been in the UK Pavilion. The ride would allow you to sit either on a bench or a carousel horse. You would enter into the animated section of the film and see various parts of it including the fox hunt, horse race, and of course singing Supercalifragilisticexpialidocious. During the ride you would see the various characters from the film. The supercalifragilisticexpialidocious segment would be the finale and at the end you would return to London and you could then go onto a Mary Poppins meet and greet.

Most likely the ride was never built for a lack of interest from any sponsors.

While Mary Poppins has not received her own ride yet, she does feature in the Great Movie Ride. Someday perhaps she will get a ride of her own.

Matterhorn

Yet again Florida would try to get their own version of the Matterhorn. This time the Disneyland classic would be located in the Switzerland section of Epcot. This version seems a bit psychedelic. While some parts of the ride seem like what you would expect in a slightly updated Matterhorn, other lighting effects seem very out of place.

The reason this Matterhorn never made it was Disney couldn't find a Swiss sponsor for the attraction.

While it would not make it out of California, the idea would be brought back as a possible ride one more time for Florida, as we will see a little later.

Meet the World

Meet the World was originally planned for the Japan Pavilion at Epcot. Meet the World was a show featuring the history of Japan shown in a circular revolving theater like Carousel of Progress. A building was made to house the show and the entire show was created.

The show found a new home in Japan. The ride also had a problem in how to deal with World War II which it simply glosses over. Disney decided that it would be better to use the show for Disneyland Japan than Epcot and they could have the Oriental Land Company pay for the show instead of Disney finding a sponsor or paying for it themselves. Meet the World was at Tokyo Disneyland until it closed and the show building torn down.

Mt. Fuji

Mt Fuji was going to be in the Japan Pavilion. The ride would be an indoor roller coaster. There were plans to house a bullet train ride as well. The ride was going to see you face down Godzilla. It would have you going from stop to stop only to see Godzilla already destroying the area or the army closing things off. Toward the end Godzilla would actually bite your train.

Unfortunately the Japanese economy crashed and Disney could not get anyone to sponsor the ride. While they tried to get Fujifilm to sponsor it, Kodak, a perennial Disney sponsor, expressed their dismay over such overtures, even the idea of a ride with a major competitor's name in it.

Mt. Fuji will likely have to remain in Japan only. For now we can only hope that somehow Godzilla makes it into the parks.

Bullet Train Ride

There were two separate locations that may have gotten a bullet train ride. Switzerland was one option. The other more likely to have received it was Japan. As mentioned, one version of the ride would have featured Godzilla. Another more peaceful version similar to a Circlevision show would let you experience the beautiful scenery of Japan without having to worry about being attacked by monsters.

The Switzerland version never was built since the Switzerland pavilion was never built. The Japanese version could not find a sponsor.

With at least three versions are known to exist, it seems like Disney really wanted to make this. For those willing to go off the beaten path there is a similar ride at Universal.

The Incredible Journey Within

The Incredible Journey Within was going to be a dark ride attraction through the human body located in the Wonders of Life Pavilion. The ride would shrink you down to allow you to go inside the human body.

The ride would have been difficult to build with the massive size of the set pieces needed to make you feel so small compared to the parts you were seeing.

The concept did evolve into Body Wars. Body Wars would take up less room and give a more thrilling ride for the older age groups.

Rhine River Cruise

The Rhine River Cruise would have been a boat ride along the famous rivers of Germany and allowed you to see miniatures of famous German landmarks.

No sponsor was found for the ride.

There is room for the ride, so maybe someday it will be built.

Thames River Ride

England could have featured the Thames River Ride. The ride would be a boat ride along the Thames River. You would see famous London landmarks on the way including Big Ben and the Tower of London.

The ride never found a sponsor.

So far, no sign of a similar ride.

Tooth Follies

Tooth Follies was a planned show for the Epcot Health Pavilion. The idea evolved into Cranium Command. Besides eventually becoming Cranium Command, the idea led to the Inside Out movie.

Christmas Carol Show

A Christmas Carol Show was planned using audio animatronic and special effects such as Pepper's Ghost for the UK Pavilion.

Most likely Disney simply could not find a sponsor. So far, no show in any of the parks are like it.

WEDway PeopleMover

Commincore and now Innoventions were designed with the intention of having a WEDWay PeopleMover installed inside.

It is likely that money was the problem that kept it from being made. Also, there would be little utility for the ride since the two are very close and as a means of transportation very impractical.

There is still room for them to be placed, but it is unlikely they ever will be.

Jr. Autopia

The Jr. Autopia was to be placed next to Test Track since Test Track would not allow children to ride even though the ride previously in the same spot allowed for it.

The most likely reason this never made it is that the sponsor of Test Track was unwilling to spend the money on it. Also, Test Track had faced many problems leading to cost overruns as well as opening late which also made it less likely that this ride would get built.

Perhaps someday a similar attraction will be built in the area for children.

Time Racers

Time Racers was going to be an indoor roller coaster that would replace Spaceship Earth. The ride would feature projections.

The main reason the ride never materialized was they decided it would be too expensive. Another problem was the difficulty of getting the ride inside Spaceship Earth.

With the popularity of Spaceship Earth and a somewhat recent upgrade, it is not likely that Time Racers will make it into Epcot any time soon.

The Land Jungle Coaster

Few details are known about the Jungle Roller Coaster which was planned for the Land Pavilion. The roller coaster would be outside and have guests ride over the canopy of a jungle in a roller coaster. The plan was part of an attempt to make Epcot more exciting. The plan was known as Project Gemini and included the previously mentioned Time Racers. The ride would have likely been a simple off-the-shelf roller coaster.

It was decided that the plan would be too expensive. Some parts of the plan did make it into the park such as the Soarin' ride.

Epcot has yet to get a roller coaster and with an educational theme may never get one. At least they have some thrills with Fast Track and Soarin'.

Tokyo Disneyland

Since Tokyo Disneyland is not owned by Disney, it does not often get rides planned just for itself. When they want a ride they often want something that has already been proven at the other parks but often upgraded. On occasion they will request new rides, but they work closely with Disney so it is rare that an idea does not get made if they start working on a concept. However, there does exist a very rare concept for an attraction that was never built in Tokyo.

UFO Encounter

Very little is known about this ride. What is known is intriguing. Guests would be captured by an audio-animatronic alien located in a giant spaceship.

Why this never made it is unknown along with most information about this ride.

While being captured by an alien sounds terrible, it is an intriguing concept that would at least be good to know more about if not see created.

Disney's Hollywood Studios

Disney's Hollywood Studios may not be that old, but because of its early success many ideas were talked about for possible rides. While the park was initially successful, it was also built near the same time that Disneyland Paris was built. With the heavy costs of Disneyland Paris, Hollywood Studio would not get the rides it might have as the money for them were tied up with Disneyland Paris. So, while it may be younger than other parks, it has a large number of unbuilt rides.

Silent Film Stunt Show

When the park first opened one plan was to have a Silent Film Stunt Show. Few details are known about this idea. However, it is likely that it would be a comical look at stunts. It is likely that it would focus on slapstick stunts such as Charlie Chaplin and Buster Keaton.

While the Silent Film Stunt Show did not make it off the page, the Indiana Jones Stunt Show was probably inspired by the idea and even replaced the concept as a more exciting alternative.

Matterhorn

The Matterhorn was a possible second phase expansion plan for Disney's Hollywood Studios. While it seems most parks have thought about adding the Disneyland classic, the Hollywood Studios version would have been a bit unique. The ride would be a facade of the Matterhorn with the back open. It would be like the facade for movies.

While it is likely that money problems caused by Disneyland Paris were partly to blame, it is also possible that someone realized that part of the magic of the Matterhorn was being inside the mountain. It is also possible other roller-coaster options such Rock 'n' Roller Coaster may have been viewed as better alternatives.

Disneyland is still the only park with a Matterhorn, but it's not for a lack of Disney trying to get the classic ride another home.

Baby Herman's Runaway Baby Buggy

Baby Herman's Runaway Baby Buggy would have been a dark ride based on the Roger Rabbit universe. The idea is that you are a stunt double for Baby Herman. You would ride in a baby buggy and go through a hair-raising ride through a hospital while playing the part of Baby Herman's stunt double.

When the Roger Rabbit's Hollywood did not get off the page, neither did the ride. There are also some legal rights issues with any of the Roger characters.

While this ride never was built, it was the inspiration for another Roger dark ride that would get built. While the Roger Rabbit's Car Toon Spin has a very different story, it is a dark ride based on Roger Rabbit.

Toontown Trolley

The Toontown Trolley ride was going to be a simulator ride that would take guests on a madcap trip through Toontown. Based on concept art, there would even be some additional effects to the ride, such as Roger Rabbit hitting and denting your trolley.

When Roger's Rabbit Hollywood didn't make it, neither did the Toontown Trolley.

The Toontown Trolley would ultimately become a ride, but not the exciting ride it could have been. Ultimately, a Toontown Trolley ride known as the Jolly Trolley would be built in Tokyo as well as at Disneyland.

Benny the Cab

Benny the Cab was going to be located in the Roger Rabbit's Hollywood section of the park. It would have been a dark ride through Toontown in Benny the Cab. The ride would have taken you outside and up the second floor of buildings during part of the ride.

Like the rest of the rides planned for Roger Rabbit's Hollywood, this ride would not be built as planned for the park because the land was never built that it was going to go to. Another problem is that the ride could not use the Benny the Cab name due to of ownership rights issues with Amblin.

While the Benny the Cab ride never came to be, a Lenny the Cab ride made it into two Disneyland theme parks. If you have ever been on Roger Rabbit's Car Toon Spin in Anaheim or Tokyo, then you have been on the Benny the Cab ride just with a new name, never going outside on the rooftops, because Disney own the full rights to the Lenny the Cab character. But other than that, it is pretty much the same ride.

Tower of Terror Alternatives

That were alternative versions of the Tower of Terror being discussed. The first idea was to have a Castle Young Frankenstein which would be more of a castle than a hotel. That shortly turned into a hotel with a variety of names including Hotel Mel and Mel Brooks' Hollywood Horror Hotel which finally gave us the idea of a hotel. An interesting idea for the ride was to have clues around the hotel that guests could find and lead to receiving a certificate if you solved the mystery. The Mel Brooks version would be a funny version.

Eventually, Mel Brooks moved on and so did the idea of a funny Tower of Terror. Mel Brooks leaving the project led to the decision to make a spookier version. A Stephen King version with a replica of the Overlook Hotel from *The Shining* was one option that was discussed. However, Disney decided that they would be limited if just working with one author's work.

One version would have a director who went mad because he couldn't make the transition from silent to talking movies. At the top of the tower you would find him as he yelled "Cut" for one last time.

None of these ideas got off the ground, but the ride ultimately would be built with a *Twilight Zone* theme instead. While Tokyo Disneyland dropped the *Twilight Zone* theme for a unique version, it is unlikely any Tower of Terror rides outside of the U.S. will use any of the earlier concepts as they would face the same problem the *Twilight Zone* had in Japan in that they would not be well known. So it is likely these ride ideas will be dropped for good.

Airplane Airport

There is not much information about the proposed Airplane Airport. What is known is that it was planned to be a massive attraction that would be very expensive.

The obvious reason the Airplane Airport was never made is that it was going to be very expensive to build.

With issues of movie rights it is unlikely that the Airplane Airport will ever land in a Disney park anytime soon.

The Great Muppet Movie Ride

The Great Muppet Movie Ride was going to be a spoof on the Great Movie Ride. The ride would take you on a similar tour as the Great Movie Ride but would feature the Muppet characters re-creating famous scenes from famous films with lots of zaniness. A Frankenstein and Peter Pan scene are known to have been planned. The cranky Statler and Waldorf would have been guests on the ride making wisecracks along the way.

The plan fell through because of the death of Jim Henson.

With Disney now owning the Muppets, it is possible that the ride could make a comeback.

The Rocketeer

The Rocketeer ride would have allowed guests to experience the feeling of flying like in *The Rocketeer* film. The ride would have been an overhead roller coaster.

Disney wanted to add more thrills and see a roller coaster built, but *The Rocketeer* did not do well enough at the box office to support a ride.

While *The Rocketeer* does have a cult following, it is unlikely that it will be enough to get this ride off the ground.

Nightmare Before Christmas Ride

A Nightmare Before Christmas Ride was proposed for the park. The ride would have been a dark ride that would have had guests board coffins. They would travel through parts of Halloween Town. They would go through the main part of town, the scientist lab, Oogie Boogies, and finally a graveyard.

During the time the film came out, there was a lot happening with the company and Disney did not have money to spend on projects that were not priorities thanks to funds being tied up in Disneyland Paris.

While there would not be an entire Nightmare Before Christmas Ride, the concept inspired the Haunted Mansion Holiday. A whole new ride could not be made to replace such a popular one, so the idea of *Nightmare Before Christmas* being featured in a ride could be done but not in the way it had originally been envisioned.

Villain Ride

At one point Disney thought of replacing the Great Movie Ride with a Villain Ride. The ride would have been in the same spot and likely used the same ride system. However this ride would feature the Disney villains in full 3D audio-animatronic glory. At the end, the Disney heroes would come and rescue you from the villains.

Why this ride never was made is unknown. One possible reason is it was going to replace a main attraction of the park.

Disney has been mulling over a ride featuring the Disney villains. It is possible at some point they will finally make such a ride and this ride could be it.

Monsters Inc. Roller Coaster

The Monsters Inc. Roller Coaster would have been an inverted roller coaster that would have simulated the scene in the movie with the doors. The ride would be a mix of dark ride and roller coaster with many different scenes. The ride would also be interactive. Instead of using a gun of some sort the interactivity would be based on how loud you scream.

No reason is known why this ride was dropped.

While this ride never made it, two dark rides themed to *Monsters Inc.* did, including one that has interactive elements using flashlights.

Disneyland Paris

As you know by now, Disneyland Paris was expected to be a huge hit. The park would bring a king's ransom to the company. However the fairy tale Disney wanted never happened. Instead Disneyland Paris ate up massive amounts of cash. Disneyland Paris ended up being responsible for many other Disney projects failing to get off the drawing boards.

As you can expect, the lack of initial success of Disneyland Paris not only caused other parks to lose out on some amazing experiences, it also meant that Disneyland Paris itself would not see many of the projects which were planned for it.

With Disneyland Paris' early initial failure to bring the expected visitors and profit for the park, many of the following rides were never built. By now you now this was the cause for so many rides, so from now on unless otherwise stated during this section just assume that the poor financial health of Disneyland Paris was to blame for the following rides failing to be built.

The Undersea Voyage of the Little Mermaid

The Undersea Voyage of the Little Mermaid was going to be a dark ride based on *The Little Mermaid*. As seen in the extras of *The Little Mermaid* DVD, the ride would bring you face-to-face with a giant Ursula near the end.

While this ride did not get built exactly as planned as shown by concept art and *The Little Mermaid* DVD, it would eventually make it into the Disney parks in a shortened version.

Main Street Elevated Tram

An elevated tram was conceived for Main Street. Guests would have been able to ride it as it passed by the stores on Main Street. It is likely that this idea went along with the 1920's era Main Street. Without a 1920s Main Street, it did not fit.

Main Street has not seen an elevated tramway, but DisneySea would have an electric railway which is very similar and likely inspired by the Main Street Elevated Tram.

Discovery Arcade Automats Museum

The Discovery Arcade Automats Museum was going to be a museum featuring classic arcade machines. These would mostly be automata from over 100 years ago.

Most likely Disney did not think there would be enough interest. Also, it can be hard to find such old machines.

While no automata museum was made, most every park has some arcades and many do have antique machines depending on the location.

Matterhorn

Once again Disney tried to bring the Matterhorn to a park outside of Disneyland.

While the financial problems of the park certainly played a role, it is also possible that with the real Matterhorn being right next door in Switzerland it would not have been very exotic or exciting.

With all the attempts Disney has made to make a second Matterhorn it may still get built somewhere, or maybe they should just build a second Matterhorn at Disneyland.

Beauty and the Beast Show

With the movie being set in France and the story being an old French fairy tale, a Beauty and the Beast show would be a perfect fit for the park. It is even odd it was not among the first shows built. The most likely reason though is that R&D can be a big part of an attraction's cost and they could use already existing attractions instead. While a cheap, fast version may have been made, concept art appears to show that Disney was going to make a technologically advanced show.

The show building would have two very different facades. The entrance would be dark and spooky, but the other side where you would exit would be more cheerful, the idea being that when you start the curse is in effect and when you exit the curse has been lifted.

The show would have used real actors mixed with animatronics. It would also have multiple scenes. The start would feature a real actress playing Belle talking with animatronic versions of the main cast of servants. You would then go to a state-of-the-art scene from the "Be Our Guest" segment. Finally, the Beast would appear. The Beast was planned to be the largest animatronic made to that time. A young female guest would be picked from the audience to give a rose to the Beast. While the show is often compared to the Tiki Room, this guest interaction makes it reminiscent of the final scene of the Cinderella Castle Mystery Tour in Tokyo. Once the child gives the Beast the rose, he would disappear and reappear as a real human prince.

Rumors have persisted for over a decade that this ride may replace another or get a whole new home. Being such a popular movie it would not be surprising to see it get made at some point. While it may not have been built as conceived, you can still see a Beauty and the Beast live show at Disney's Hollywood Studios.

Doc's Driving School

Doc's Driving School was planned to open with the Walt Disney Studios Park. The idea would be that you were being taught by Doc how to be a race car driver. The ride may have been similar to Test Track and Radiators Springs Racers. The theme and many scenes would have been different from the Radiator

Springs Racers, however. It is possible it may have been a clone of the track.

The Walt Disney Studios Park faced many cutbacks and Doc's Driving School was one of the projects that would not make the cut.

The Radiator Springs Racers would be similar to Doc's Driving School. If the idea for Doc's came first, then it is likely the inspiration for Radiator Springs Racers.

Splash Mountain

Splash Mountain would have been a clone of the already popular attractions in the other parks.

While cost was one problem, the other was that it gets cold in Paris and Disney decided it would not be a good idea to have a ride where you could get wet in the middle of a Parisian winter.

Because of the weather, it is unlikely that Disneyland Paris will get Splash Mountain.

Geyser Mountain

Geyser Mountain would have been the same as the previously mentioned Geyser Mountain for Disneyland.

Since the Disneyland Paris Resort ended up getting the Twillight Zone Tower of Terror, it is unlikely that it will get a re-themed version of the ride.

Tarzan Coaster

The Tarzan Coaster would have you experience what it is like to be Tarzan flying though the trees. The ride would be built by the pirate ship and go around the Swiss Family Treehouse.

This would not be the first time a Tarzan roller coaster has been suggested. It is possible that Tarzan will get a roller coaster. But Tarzan did get his own Treehouse at Disneyland.

Second Indiana Jones Temple Coaster

A second roller coaster near the first Indiana Jones roller coaster was planned. Little is known about how this roller coaster would have been different.

It is unlikely that this coaster made it to any other park. Also, with such little information it is hard to know if a brand new roller coaster was made that it was inspired by this buried idea.

Disney's Animal Kingdom

Disney's Animal Kingdom is physically the largest of all the parks. This has given it ample space to see many ideas come and go. While it is a newer park compared to many, the space along with its special requirements owing to live animals being present has meant a large number of ride ideas would not be able to be used.

Animal Kingdom was Disney's first attempt at making a theme park with real animals. Disney learned a number of things they had not expected during the construction. Issues of noise for the animals was a concern in some cases. A major concern is that a good amount of the cost is on taking care of the animals, housing them, etc. Most of the money for the park would go into what is behind the scenes that the guests never get to see. This limited what could be built with the budget they had originally set aside.

Dragon Tower

The Dragon Tower would be a roller-coaster ride in the Beastly Kingdom section of the park. Bats would recruit you to help them steal the treasure from the dragon. The ride would have you go face to face with a fire-breathing animatronic dragon.

The Beastly Kingdom section of the park was scrapped and so was the ride.

While Dragon Tower was never made at a Disney park, according to a persistent rumor the Imagineers who left Disney to go to work for Universal took the idea and made the Dueling Dragons coaster at Islands of Adventure.

Quest for the Unicorn

The Quest for the Unicorn was another planned attraction for Beastly Kingdom. Guests would enter a hedge maze. The Quest for the Unicorn would be a walk-through attraction similar to the Disneyland Paris Alice Labyrinth. The attraction would have many mythological creatures that would help you on your way through the maze. The finale would be where you see the unicorn. The unicorn would be able to telepathically talk to you by way of hidden speakers; this was done because the Imagineers had a hard time figuring out a way to make the unicorn talk without it looking odd.

Obviously, with Beastly Kingdom not making it, the Quest for the Unicorn was a lost quest. Other problems, though, would have made it difficult. There were concerns over crowd control and how to handle a large number of guests in a walk-through attraction. Another major concern is it would have taken a long time to grow the plants necessary for the planned attraction.

With a strong emphasis on guests per hour for attractions and the long time needed to grow the plants to the needed sizes, it may be that the Quest for the Unicorn will never be more then a Disney legend.

Fantasia Gardens

Fantasia Gardens was going to be a boat ride through scenes from the movie *Fantasia*. The boat ride would focus on the section of the movie featuring mythical creatures such as centaurs. Other scenes that would be included include the dancing hippos and alligators.

This ride was never built because the Beastly Kingdom section it would have been located in was never built.

A Fantasia Gardens did open with a *Fantasia* theme, but it is a mini golf course. However, it is possible that the golf course was inspired by this ride as Disney never gets rid of good ideas.

Enhanced DINOSAUR

The original plans for the DINOSAUR ride were more involved and are often referred to as the Enhanced DINOSAUR ride. The ride vehicles would be shaped like an anklyosaurus. The ride would feature a number of extra scenes including a T-Rex, a volcano, being attacked, and more scenes that did not make it into the current version of the ride.

The likely cause for the cutbacks to the ride were financial.

The ride did open, but it was not as impressive as originally planned. Not only did it not live up to the original plans, but because of technical problems the experience that guests get now from what was offered when the ride first opened has also been watered down.

Tarzan Rainforest Roller Coaster

The Tarzan Rainforest Roller Coaster would have been an inverted coaster through the jungle.

The ride likely never was built due to budget reasons.

A similar concept was mentioned for the Land Pavilion in Epcot which also did not fly off the page. Tarzan would get a show for a time at Animal Kingdom and has his tree house in Disneyland. However, for now we will just have to wait to experience what it is like to be Tarzan and fly through the trees.

The Excavator

The Excavator was going to be a roller coaster that would open with the park in the Dinoland area. Many pieces of concept art exist. The ride would be a mine car roller coaster through a dinosaur dig site.

The ride was cut due to budget reasons. The space planned for it would get Primeval Whirl and TriceraTop Spin. Disney decided it would be cheaper to take an off-the-shelf ride like Primeval Whirl and add some thematic pieces than to make an entire new E-ticket attraction for a land that already had one.

With the space taken for the ride gone, it is unlikely this ride will be dug up any time soon.

Dinorama Meteor Dark Ride

The Dinorama Meteor Dark Ride would be a dark ride similar to DINOSAUR but for kids. The ride would be less scary. It would give those that couldn't go on DINOSAUR a chance to get up close to dinosaurs. After all, it's the little kids that love dinosaurs the most, but they are the ones not able to ride DINOSAUR.

It was budget problems that made this ride extinct.

The entire park is popular with children since it is about animals which children love. Since it was just a children's version of a ride in the park, it is unlikely to have a reason to be placed anywhere else. The park already has plenty for kids even in the area, so it is likely this ride will remain extinct.

The Tree of Life Carousel

The Tree of Life Carousel would have been the park's wienie. It would have been a three-tiered carousel featuring lots of different animals. The ride would feature a first floor of boats or animals from the water, the second would be animals on land, while the third would be animals in the air and would allow guests to control the flights like the Dumbo ride.

Money was not the reason this concept never took root. Being the centerpiece for the park it had an important position. It was decided that it was not the best option for the spot.

It is unlikely Disney will have the need of this kind of ride as it was meant to be special to Animal Kingdom as its centerpiece attraction.

Tree of Life Shows

A variety of shows were under consideration for the Tree of Life theater. Some shows under discussion included a Lion King show and a show featuring Mother Nature.

Mother Nature was probably viewed as to boring and not worthy of the spot. Lion King may have been viewed as being to old or there may have been concern about the Magic Kingdom having a Lion King show already at the time. Ultimately, Disney preferred It's Tough to Be a Bug.

It is hard to say if these ever will get made as little information on the content of the shows are known. However, the Tree of Life did get a show inside of it as planned. Perhaps when Disney decided they need a new show one of these could replace the current one.

Tiger River Rapids

Tiger River Rapids was the original version of Kali River Rapids. The main difference was that it would have been much larger in scale. Tiger River Rapids was going to be close to the size of the Kilimanjaro Safari ride. The ride would have focused on Asia, Asian animals, and tigers in particular.

Most likely the ride was cut back because of costs. Animal Kingdom was a surprise for Disney since they never worked with animals and did not realize so much of the budget would be spent on the unseen necessities of animal care.

The ride did get made but on a much smaller scale as Kali River Rapids.

Disney California Adventure

For being such a new park, Disney's California Adventure has lots of rides that never were made. One main reason for this is that the park was often criticized when it first opened. It was viewed as a mini park and a way for Disney to make a quick buck off tourists.

When Bob Iger took over the company he decided that he would fix the park before building a new park. So Disney decided to spend more to work on a huge expansion of the park. This expansion was like building a whole new park in terms of ideas. Plus the ideas could be done quickly and cheaply over actually creating any of them. So the best ideas would be built and the rest would be forgotten dreams.

Rock 'n' Roller Coaster Starring No Doubt

Assuming it would fit, this would be a clone of Rock 'n' Roller Coaster at Disney's Hollywood Studio but feature a soundtrack featuring the Anaheim-based band No Doubt. Some claim this was going to be located where Golden Dreams was to be made.

This ride was likely never built due to budget constraints. They also would have had to get the band's approval. While No Doubt members are Disney fans, they also can be a bit skeptical of the company as can be heard from their song "Tragic Kingdom." It is also possible that Disney may have objected to the group because of the song's opening: "Once was a magical place over time it was lost." The entire song is a parody on Disney and while it comes across that they like the old Disney, the new Disney is now run by "jesterly fools." The song which was also the title of the band's first album may not have ingratiated them with the company if they had taken the time to listen to their music.

So far, only one new Rock 'n' Roller Coasters has been built. It is possible more will be in the future. But it is doubtful that they will feature No Doubt.

Chocolate Factory Tour

The park originally planned to have a Chocolate Factory Tour. The tour would have included a free sample of chocolate at the end.

It is likely that there was only room for so many similar attractions and Boudin Bread and Mission Tortilla had more interest than a chocolate company.

After the Mission Tortilla company did not renew the lease, a Ghirardelli store was put in its place. They do offer a free sample of chocolate, but there is no factory tour.

Golden Dreams

There is a Golden Dream show, but it is a far cry from the original plan for the show. Had the show been made as originally planned, it still might be at the park.

A CircleVision film was planned which would include animatronics similar to the Timekeeper but on a larger scale. Ultimately, cuts were made and it was to become a regular movie with animatronics. Even with these cuts, it was decided more cuts needed to be made and it was cut down to just a movie. It was cut back so much that even Whoopi Goldberg is reported to have complained to Michael Eisner about it.

The movie never made much of an impact. It is unlikely that an improved, more expensive version will ever be produced.

Grizzly Railroad

Grizzly Railroad was planned for the Grizzly Peak area of California Adventure. There seems to be some debate over whether it was to be purely scenic or a roller coaster, although if it had been a roller coaster, most accounts claim it would have been a more family friendly one.

By now you probably think you know why it was never built. If you said money, you would actually be wrong this time. The real reason was space. There is no space for it in the area. More recently, a similar idea with a Gold Rush-themed train ride was considered, but it was rejected because the infrastructure of the mountain would not make it possible.

The idea would get used in Hong Kong as the Big Grizzly Mountain Runaway Mine Cars.

Country Bear Jamboree

Disneyland did have a Country Bear Jamboree. The show was removed to make room for Winnie the Pooh. In a classic example of how sometimes things that work on one coast do not work on another, the Pooh ride was not particularly popular. In fact, one of the best things about the ride is if the park is crowded you still can get on without much wait.

Bringing back Country Bear Jamboree to Disneyland would be a great idea as many fans were sad to see it go. Being a show, it could accommodate many people and on hot summer days get people out of the heat. The location seems perfect in Grizzly Peak except for one flaw: there is no room. When Disney was thinking about adding in a mine train, they also thought of adding in a new Country Bear Jamboree.

Like the mine train, even the Country Bear Jamboree would not have room in the area.

Had it been brought back, it would not be the first time an attraction returned. Captain EO would return to its original location. Also, the Main Street Electrical Parade spent time in California Adventure after it had left Disneyland so it would not be the first time that something closed at Disneyland only to move next door to California Adventure.

Paradise Pier Water Flume

Yet again Disney had an idea for a shoot-the-chutes ride that would end up not making it. The ride would have been a typical shoot-the-chutes water ride going up a ramp and turning around only to drop guests into the Paradise Pier bay.

While budget cuts were a part of the demise of this attraction, the main problem was getting it to fit. Not putting this ride in may have been a good thing for Disney. With the World of Color using the lagoon, something would have had to been done with the ride including possibly closing it or closing it during the show.

It is now unlikely that it will ever be built in the same spot in California Adventure because of the World of Color show. Since the idea keeps coming up so often with Disney, it may just be a matter of time until Disney finally uses this classic theme park attraction.

The Walt Disney Story

The Walt Disney Story would have been a movie about Walt Disney and in particular his history with the state of California.

This is one of those rare times when money was not the main problem keeping an attraction from opening. A show would have been a cheap way to keep lots of people busy. The reason it was canceled was it was decided that the park already had too many shows such as Golden Dreams, It's Tough to Be a Bug, and Muppet*Vision 3-D.

It was probably a good decision, but for Disney fans it may have been better to leave one of the other shows out and let this show get made.

Green Army Men Parachute Drop

The Green Army Men Parachute Drop was going to be part of the California Adventure expansion. The ride was going to be a refurbishment of the Mailboomer.

With that expansion, as previously mentioned, Toy Story Pier was an idea and the Green Army Men Parachute Drop would have been a part of that. The decision to cut down on Toy Story was part of the reason this ride never made it. The other reason was that it was too similar to the Tower of Terror.

The ride did make into the Walt Disney Studios Park and Hong Kong Disneyland.

Ursula Spinner

A spinning ride was to feature a giant Ursula holding onto bottles and other over-sized vehicles in each tentacle. The ride would be located near the exit of California Screamin' and King Triton's Carousel.

No reason for the ride failing to be built is known, but the cost overruns fo the park may have been to blame.

While Ursula did not get her own ride, a Little Mermaid ride would get built in DCA across the lake about 180 degrees from where Ursula would have been.

Monsters Inc. Roller Coaster

A Monsters Inc. Roller Coaster was planned for the spot where the Muppets show is. The ride would have been based on the movie scene with all the doors.

It is likely that Disney's more recent and profitable acquisitions made them decide to go with other properties first, so a Mosnters Inc. roller coaster was not such a high-flying plan.

Zurg

The Zurg ride was going to be called just Zurg. It would be another simple overlay of an already existing ride. Zurg would have replaced the Golden Zephyr.

The reason it was canceled was Disney felt that the land already had to many Toy Story-themed attractions in the area and did not want to add any more.

It is unlikely that this will ever get built in the future as it would need a reason like an entire Toy Story land and a pre-existing ride it could replace.

Mickey's PhilharMagic

Mickey's PhilharMagic was planned to replace the Muppet*Vision 3D show. The show would have been the same as the one featured at the Magic Kingdom.

The problem was the show system did not fit into the existing theater and major refurbishment would have to be done on the theater for the show to fit. Disney decided it was not worth the effort to change it.

While Muppet*Vision 3D is safe for now, it seems to be in the cross-hairs of Disney and once a popular show does come around that would fit into the theater it may be the end of the Muppets for good.

Toy Story the Musical

Toy Story the Musical was planned for California Adventure. It would have been in the Hyperion theater even though it was to be associated with Toy Story Land. It was announced but later canceled.

It is likely the reason it was canceled is that the Toy Story theming never made it. Also, it was not even physically connected to the land.

Toy Story the Musical did make it onto the Disney *Wonder*, however.

Road Trip USA

Road Trip USA was to be the main attraction in the originally planned Carland. The ride may have been based off the Test Track system like the eventual Radiator Racers. Or it may have just been a simple car ride. The ride would have been a zany trip through cheesy tourist traps. The ride would have been at least partially but probably mostly outside. You would see all kinds of wacky kitsch along the way.

While budget constraints were a reason this ride never made it, one of the biggest problems that Disney had with the ride and land as we discussed before was its lack of Disney characters. It was a lack of synergy with the company's pre-existing product that kept this ride from happening.

The Imagineers and the company loved the idea, though, and it stayed around. Finally, after the popularity of the movie *Cars*, it was realized they now had a Disney property that would fit the idea. While changes were made to fit Carland with the property, Carsland does owe Carland a debt of gratitude. Road Trip USA may never become a ride, but Radiator Racers would.

Geppetto's Workshop

Geppetto's Workshop was not a new ride but a new overlay on the Orange Stinger. While Disney would change the Orange Stinger, it would choose to go with a Mickey Mouse version instead.

So the Orange Stinger would get a new overlay but not to Geppetto. It is unlikely that Geppetto's Workshop will get made as it was just out of a need to change an already existing ride easily.

Armageddon Special Effects

Armageddon Special Effects would be a special-effects show at California Adventures based around the movie *Armageddon*. The spot ended up going to Who

Wants to be a Millionaire? It is likely that it had to do both with cost as well as the relative popularity of the two projects.

The show would make it to Paris, however.

Incredibles

Few details are known about the Incredibles ride. One thing that is known is that it would have used the same new ride technology seen on the Harry Potter and the Forbidden Journey ride in Orlando. Disney decided to make Carsland instead of an Incredibles land since the *Cars* movies were more popular.

A ride using the same technology is likely to be built since it has been so popular in Islands of Adventure. But *Incredibles* is an older movie now that did not have the same success as other films so it may not happen.

Tokyo DisneySea

Since Tokyo DisneySea is one of the newest Disney parks, it has not had time to see many ideas come and go. Also, since it is not owned directly by Disney, rides for it are not a priority. Also, Disney does not have to foot the bill for any rides, so often a ride suggested will end up being made. The working relationship with the Oriental Land Company is different and it helps keep unrealized plans to a minimum.

The Undersea Voyage of the Little Mermaid

This would have been a dark ride for the Mermaid Lagoon section. Had it been built it would have been the first Little Mermaid dark ride.

It is not known why this ride was not built.

This ride would eventually get built in multiple parks.

The Jungle Book Audio-Animatronic Show

The Jungle Book Audio Animatronic Show would have been what it sounds like, a show featuring audio-animatronic *Jungle Book* characters. It is likely it would have been placed in the Lost River Delta.

No reason is known why it was never built.

Had the live-action movie been a huge hit, it may have sparked interest in the original movie which may have given this a new lease on life. For now, *Jungle Book* fans will have to wait.

SS Columbia Showcase of Nautical Marvels

The SS Columbia Showcase of Nautical Marvels was going to be what is known as a madhouse ride. It would be a round theater that appears to swing and move around you. The story would be that you were boarding a ship that used state-of-the-art gyroscopes to give you the smoothest sea voyage in the world. However, something goes wrong and you end up having one of the roughest voyages instead.

The Oriental Land Company didn't feel that the ride was particularly impressive and only wanted to include top-notch rides for the new park.

This is actually a popular classic attraction that Disney has never used, so perhaps in time Disney will find a way to use it.

Cops and Robbers Chase and Beagle Boys

The Cops and Robbers Chase would have featured two separate tracks. Guests would either be cops or robbers. The ride itself would be a crazy mouse-style roller coaster. An alternative version would feature the Beagle Boys as the robbers.

This is another example of a ride being turned down because it did not meet the high expectations for the new park.

Other mouse-style coasters have made it into the Disney parks, but this particular theme may not get out of jail any time soon.

Manhattan Motor Mania

The Manhattan Motor Mania would be a dark ride with outdoor elements. It would be similar to Mr Toad's Wild Ride but through New York in slightly larger cars. Another suggestion for this ride was to include the Muppets in it.

Again the top brass at the Oriental Land Company were not impressed. Even with the Muppets it was not unique enough for them.

This is another situation where the ride just fit the area so it is unlikely this ride will get another run at reality, but you never know with Disney.

Lighthouse of Alexandria

Because Japan is not as familiar with the *Twilight Zone*, Disney came up with some other concepts to bring the ride into the park. The Lighthouse of Alexandria was one of these ideas.

Ultimately, the Lighthouse of Alexandria lost out to the current version at DisneySea.

The Lighthouse of Alexandria was not built, but the ride that it would have housed was.

Hong Kong Disneyland

As we discussed earlier when talking about lands, Hong Kong Disneyland has an inordinate number of unbuilt attractions for its young age. We already discussed the reasons for the large number of lands. With more lands come more rides. So the large number of attractions that have gone unbuilt for this park is for the same reasons as the large number of unrealized lands.

The Little Mermaid: Ariel's Undersea Adventure

This was yet another time Disney tried to get a Little Mermaid dark ride built. The ride would be the same as all the others around the world.

The ride is located in other parks.

Peter Pan's Flight

The Peter Pan's Flight would have been very similar to the one featured in the Magic Kingdom.

We do not know why this ride never flew off the page, but it is likely that it was a money issue.

Other Peter Pan's Flights exist and new ones still get built such as the Shanghai Disneyland version so next time Disney makes a park it is very likely that Peter Pan's Flight will once more take flight.

Raging Spirits

With the same name it is likely this would have been a clone of the DisneySea ride of the same name. The ride would for sure have been a roller coaster.

No reason is known for this ride never running, but it is likely that money was the cause.

Raging Spirits has already been made once and it is

possible it could be made again, but hopefully Disney will do something new instead.

The Boneyard

The Boneyard would have been a clone of the one in Animal Kingdom. It would be a place for kids to explore.

It is hard to say why this never made it as it would have been fairly cheap as attractions go. It is possible it was a cultural issue; perhaps the local authorities thought kids digging up dinosaur bones was not appropriate for some reason.

So far only one Boneyard exists, but if there is a place to put a new one it may not stay extinct for long.

Raft Ride

A raft ride which is believed to be a clone of the one at California Adventure was planned. It is likely it would have been located in Grizzly Gulch.

No reason is known for the ride not getting made.

Raft rides seem to be popular in recent years with Disney, so another raft ride may pop up soon.

Toy Story Mania

Toy Story Mania would have been located in Toy Story Land. It would have been a clone of the popular attraction located in other Disney parks.

With the popularity of the attraction, it is hard to understand why the ride did not get built. It is possible that the government which has a stake in the park did not like the idea of a shooting ride.

Toy Story Mania is already in most Disney resorts so there are few spots left to add it unless in a new park.

Star Tours

Disneyland Hong Kong would have had a Star Tours clone.

Likely the reason they did not make the ride is they wanted something new and unique and instead of Star Tours they are getting the Iron Man Experience.

Star Tours still could make it into China; it just may have to be the mainland.

Pirates of the Caribbean

While Pirates of the Caribbean is at every other Disney resort, the one at Disneyland Hong Kong would have been unique. It is likely it would be more focused on the movie than the original ride. It also was going to have a large drop like Splash Mountain.

The main reason this ride never was built is that it would have had its own land, the Isla Tortuga previously mentioned. Since the land did not get built, the ride did not have a land to be built in.

Some of the concepts are said to have gone into the Shanghai Disneyland ride.

Soarin'

A Soarin' ride was planned for Tomorrowland. The ride would have been the same as at other parks.

It is not a Hong Kong original and existed in other locations. However, Soarin' would make it to China.

Fort Adventures

A dark ride to be placed in a fort was being planned. Little information is known about it.

It is probable that this ride was going to be a part of Frontierland. Since Frontierland was not built, the ride did not get built.

Restaurants

Restaurants may not be the sexiest of projects to work on, but they are a necessary part of the experience. Without restaurants you would could not stay at the park all day. Without them at the resorts you would have to go off property to get food when the parks close.

Restaurants help carry the theme. They are one component of what makes Disney different than the other theme parks. Think of the food you like to eat and the places you like to eat at Disney. Now think of the places and foods at other parks. You might have a favorite food somewhere else like if you are a southern Californian then maybe a Berry Juice at Knott's Berry Juice, but does a location to get them stand out? Looking at Knott's, even their main restaurant which is popular has good food but is it themed to the Disney level?

Most theme parks probably don't even have a place you can think of to eat. That may be changing a little, but it is still limited. With Disney, even generic food such as a hot dog is sold in a way that makes it unique and special. Just look at Mickey's Toontown and Pluto's Dog House.

We all have special places to eat at the park. Some have a special food and some have a special snack. I like to get a Dole Whip Float right before the Tiki Room show starts and eat it during the show and then quietly head out once I am finished. No other attraction lets you eat in the attraction like that. For some it's the theme, for others it's the food. At Disney World I love the Sci-Fi Dine In. The food is not that good, but the experience is fun and you can't get it anywhere else except maybe an actual drive in, but there are not many of those left.

So while they may not be why you go to the park, restaurants are something that you will be looking forward to when you arrive. Restaurants are something that makes Disney stand out from everyone else. You never really leave the magic. Other locations break you out of the magic of location to get food but not with Disney. While the taste may be a part of the experience with Disney, even average food can be an experience because of the restaurant.

Disneyland

There have been a couple of restaurant ideas for the Disneyland park that never made it. Both are connected together and both would ultimately be the seed of an idea that would make it into the park.

Confucius Restaurant

The Confucius Restaurant was planned to be a part of Disneyland's Chinatown which was discussed earlier. It was to be a Chinese food restaurant. What would make the Confucius Restaurant so memorable would be the use of an audio-animatronic Confucius. Many may be surprised to learn that this was actually before Mr. Lincoln. It was just after the second attempt at an animtraonic and the first life-sized audio-animatronic based on a human.

The Confucius Restaurant started out without the animatronic as just a Chinese restaurant as a way to showcase other ethnic groups of California. However, once work on the Confucius figure began, Walt was so impressed he wanted it to be included, and even an animatronic dragon was to be added as well. After the dragon was added, it was decided that audio-animatronic birds would also be added.

The audio-animatronic Confucius only ever made it so far as a head, but it was an early and often overlooked piece of animatronic Disney history. The Imagineers liked the idea of using Confucius for a variety of reasons. First, he was old so he would not be expected to move much and could simply sit down. Second, he could wear baggy silk clothes which would not look out of place but would allow for more room for the mechanics inside.

While Chinatown and the Confucius Restaurant would not make it off the drawing board, the animatronic idea would. Also, as we already discussed, Confucius would directly lead to a president audio-animatronic which would end up being Mr. Lincoln. While the Confucius Restaurant may not have been built yet, as Confucius said the trip of 1000 miles begins with a first step.

The Tiki Hut

The original idea for the Tiki Room was not just a show but a full restaurant and show. The idea was to have a restaurant where audio-animatronic birds would put on a show for you while you ate. It was thought it would be easier to control an animatronic bird than a human, like Confucius.

One concern that was brought up with the idea of a restaurant with birds, even mechanical ones, was that people may not realize they were fake and be worried about the sanitation. But the most often-cited problem is that people would come in at various times and miss the show. You could have a set time for a show to start and bring in guests at the start of the show. The problem with that is people eat at different speeds.

When Walt decided that a dinner would not work, he scrapped the idea for the restaurant but kept the idea of the bird show. That show would become the Tiki Room. To this day you are allowed to eat in the Tiki Room. The line is faster to get Dole Whip, but you have to time it right so you get in shortly after getting your food or you will be stuck waiting for the next show and you probably wont have any food left for the show. Conveniently, the doors are also unlocked and you are allowed to leave early if you want.

Walt Disney World's Magic Kingdom

One restaurant was proposed and failed to get built at the Magic Kingdom.

Astronomers Club

The Astronomers Club was going to be built in Tomorrowland. It would have been similar to the Explorers Club in Pleasure Island, but it would have had a retro-science feel to fit with the new Tomorrowland theme. It would have been located next to the Timekeeper and have featured the robot from the show.

Most likely this never made it because it would have been too much to do. Often new projects get scaled back as costs go up. It is likely this was just a scale back from the changes made to Tomorrowland.

So far, no Astronmers Club has opened and it is not likely to happen.

Disney's Hollywood Studios

There were two restaurants that were being considered for Disney's Hollywood Studios. Neither made it.

David's Copperfield Magic Underground

David Copperfield's Magic Underground got as far as being given a billboard and an opening date of summer 1998. The project never even started construction. Disney was not going to be the only location to get a Copperfield Magic Underground. The first planned location would be in New York.

The restaurant sounds like it would have been amazing with tables magically appearing for you. If only they would do that as soon as you walked in, but I have a feeling those magic tables may take some time to appear. Guests would be able to be involved in various magic tricks.

The big problem was that David Copperfield wanted everything perfect. He had his name and reputation riding on this. If the restaurant did not provide guests with a good show, it would hurt his reputation even though he was not there. A magic show where audiences are given a limited viewing angle and perspective is a problem when trying to do magic. Not only did Copperfield expect the tricks to work and the tricks not be revealed, but he expected to allow everyone a good view of the trick. This added a whole new level of difficulty to the project.

Had Copperfield Magic Underground been a hit it was also planned to get a place at the Disneyland Resort, and even make its way to Tokyo Disney. Unfortunately, the very first location in New York never opened and the company declared bankruptcy. So don't expect Copperfield Magic Underground to appear anytime soon.

Gonzo's Pandemonium Pizza Parlor

As you may have already guessed from the name, Gonzo's Pandemonium Pizza Parlor was going to be a pizza parlor that was run by Gonzo of Muppets fame. Plans included a track system for mice to bring you your food. Gonzo going through the air ducts. Pandemonium being heard and occasionally seen in the kitchen with effects of smoke or even occasional feathers flying from out of the kitchen.

The main reason this never worked was it was to be part of the Muppets land that never got built. However, even had that are been built there are other problems it may have faced. Some obvious problems are that Rizzo a rat was to be an owner and a rat in a kitchen may not be what patrons want to think about. The same goes for rats giving you your food.

Disneyland Paris

We now come to the last of the restaurants that never got built. This time we will be looking at restaurants that were meant for Disneyland Paris.

Nautilus Restaurant

The Nautilus Restaurant was planned to be an undersea-themed restaurant that would be inside the *Nautilus*. Captain Nemo's organ would be at one end of the restaurant and on the sides and above you would be windows to look into the water.

Possible reasons it was not made are that it was turned into the walk-through instead since that has the Nemo Organ in it. It would be odd to have two organs. Another likely reason was a lack of funds.

Main Street Art Deco Restaurant

The Main Street Art Deco Restaurant was planned to have an Art Deco theme. The restaurant would be behind the transportation building. The idea for the restaurant was that you were dinning on an upscale train. It was planned to be similar to Club 33 and only available to members.

Since the park did not start off well, there was little reason to think that there would be interest in a exclusive private members-only restaurant. It is likely that it was planned to be built in a later phase once Disney knew if there would be interest.

Hotels

Since Disney has major tourist destinations where people will come from all over the world, they need to have somewhere to put them. So they build hotels. Sometimes Disney plans hotels that never get built. While this may not be the most glamorous area of the forgotten world, it still deserves coverage.

Disneyland

Walt knew at the very start that he would need a hotel. He barely had enough money to make his own hotel, so he had to literally beg his friend Jack Wrather to make a hotel instead. With an already existing hotel and little room for expansion, Disneyland would not see many ideas for a hotel.

Disneyland Resort Hotel

The Disneyland Resort Hotel was going to be an 800-room complex. The look would be based on the famous Hotel del Coronado. The hotel was never built. It is likely that money and space were both reasons this hotel never was built.

Magic Kingdom Hotel

Little is known about this besides that it would be located in Downtown Disney and was to be styled after the Santa Barbara Mission.

Walt Disney World

Being a much larger property with plenty of room for growth and having many theme parks and attractions on property, Disney World requires more hotels. Since it needs them and has room, it is able to make more. It also plans more which do not get built for various reasons as well.

Main Street USA Hotel

When the Magic Kingdom was first planned, it was going to have a hotel in the park on Main Street. The reason this hotel was never built is they couldn't figure out how to have a hotel inside the park.

This idea would resurface a few times. Eventually, Disneyland Paris would build a hotel over the turnstiles in Disneyland Paris. California Adventure would also get a hotel right next to it. Finally, the Tokyo DisneySea Hotel Mira Costa would be entirely in a Disney park.

Disney's Asian Resort

Disney's Asian Resort would have been a resort hotel adjacent to the Magic Kingdom that would have been themed to Asia. Construction went so far as to build a foundation. The project was halted because of low park attendance due to the energy crisis.

Disney's Venetian Resort

Disney's Venetian Resort was to be another resort on the Seven Seas Lagoon which was to be near the Transportation and Ticket Center. The hotel was to have a Venetian theme. Land was cleared but the area was not suitable as it was discovered to be marshy and would have required too much work.

Disney's Persian Resort

Disney's Persian Resort would also have been in the Seven Seas Lagoon area. It would have had a Persian theme. The resort was going to be funded by the Shah of Iran, but the overthrow of the Shah ended the chance that it would be built.

Disney's Mediterranean Resort

Disney's Mediterranean Resort would also be on the Seven Seas Lagoon. It was to have a Greek theme. It was going to be located where the Venetian was. It could not be built because of bad ground conditions.

Cypress Point Lodge

The Cypress Point Lodge was to have an outdoors theme. While the oil embargo kept the Cypress Point Lodge from being built, it would ultimately get built later with some modifications as Wilderness Lodge.

Fort Wilderness Junction

Themed to the Old West, the Fort Wilderness Junction would have been similar to the Disneyland Paris Cheyenne Hotel and feature the Buffalo Bill Wild West Show. The hotel would feature its own train which would take guests to multiple locations in the resort.

The economic slow down and the poor performance of Disneyland Paris would hog tie this project.

Pop Century

You may be saying there is a Pop Century resort. There is, but it is only half of the resort that was planned. The first 50 years of the century would have been featured, too. Most of the resort was built sans the thematic elements and even some of those were built.

However, the economy was slow during the time and the 9/11 attacks slowed travel even more. So the project was put on hold. For years guests could see the unfinished shell of the planned second phase and even walk across a bridge to the area before being blocked from getting closer.

Ultimately, the economy got better and demand for more hotels grew. However, the theme was not well received as it lacked the Disney touch so the new hotels would be Disney-inspired instead and would become the Art of Animation resort using the buildings but with a whole new look.

Mousellaneous

There are many projects that Disney worked on that are hard to categorize. When Walt was in charge, the company did what he wanted. Walt liked to do new things. But with his death, the company tends to stay with what they know and not branch out. So, many of the more unique ideas on this list are from Walt while less unique but hard-to-define ideas came later.

Tiki Costumes

Costume characters are nothing new to Disney, but most of the characters in the park are from Disney animated movies. The Tiki costumes would have seen costumed characters based on the Tiki Room show. A number of Tiki costumes were designed but never built.

There is something about the Tiki Room getting its own costumes because eventually Disney World would get a costumed Orange Bird for the Florida Tiki Room. The Country Bears would get costumes. Later Haunted Mansion characters would also get costumes, but they would rarely be seen. So if anyone has problems with Orange Bird or other ride-based characters, just remember the idea for a ride specific costume was born when Walt was around.

Mineral King Resort

This is a project that is unique because it was not going to be located at a Disney theme park. The resort would be located in Mineral King, a valley in the Sequoia national park. The resort would be a ski resort. It would feature ski runs, a hotel, and even a restaurant with an audio-animatronic show. The audio-animatronic show that was being planned would feature singing bears. Many announcements and plans were made to open the resort.

Walt was an avid outdoor and winter sports fan. He was a major influence in the popularity and success of the Squaw Valley Olympics. He had visited Mineral King before and loved it. Walt wanted to change ski resorts like he had changed theme parks and used Mineral King as his starting point.

The Mineral King project faced many challenges. A road would be needed to be built to access the area. The government was a great help to Disney making the initial deal as well as going through the process to get a road built. The problem came from environmental groups that did not approve. Disney faced many legal battles against the resort. He made changes such as using a cog railroad to get access to the resort instead of cars going all the way up. Disney continually cut back the size of the project as well. Walt died before the project could begin construction. While the company continued to fight the legal opposition, they ultimately gave up on the project instead of continuing to fight.

The audio-animatronic bear show would end up in theme parks around the world as the Country Bear Jamboree.

Epcot

There is an Epcot, but it is nothing like the Epcot that Walt had dreamed of. Walt was interested in urban planning and development as well as being a believer in the great potential for progress for mankind, thanks to science. Walt was a product of his time. When Walt was born, man had not even flown. In his life he would see such amazing advancements so quickly that it is no surprise he held such beliefs. The subject of Epcot is so big that it literally has filled a book.

Walt wanted to build a cutting edge city of the future, not just a theme park. He wanted to have people live and work in the city. The city would be built according to modern ideas of urban planning. Epcot would be circular with the center being the heart of commerce. High density areas would follow. Finally, a green belt would have lower density living areas as well as parks and other community-based areas.

Transportation would be by monorail and PeopleMover. Cars would be located underneath the town, keeping pedestrians safe. No one would own land, they would only rent, but rent would be kept low. Upgrades and improvements would be constant as improved technology came about.

Epcot was never built for many reasons. The main reason it was never realized was Walt Disney died before he could start to build it. While it is hard to imagine such a city being created and working, Walt is the one person repeatedly proved he could do what others thought was impossible.

Had Walt lived, many problems would have existed. The cost would have been enormous. The road system would have cost a fortune to put everything below ground. Monorails are very expensive. The transportation system would have been a headache to create even if it would have been great to live with once finished.

It would have been expensive to build such a large urban center. Places like Downtown Disney are not entire cities just small shopping areas. Walt wanted a whole city. He also wanted to bring in companies to come and create. Companies were probably not too keen on having a vast majority of their research and development in one place and certainly wouldn't have wanted to share what they were working on.

People also may not like living in a place they couldn't own. While Walt thought he could create a place where slums could not pop up because he would not let them, he could not control people. He planned to not let people who did not work live in the city. What happens with retirees? Would they try to kick out someone that did not work? That would be asking for a lawsuit. Epcot may have been a rare time when Walt did not fully understand what people wanted.

Epcot would be built as a theme park. It would have little resemblance to the plan Walt had. A model of the planned Epcot can be seen on the PeopleMover in the Magic Kingdom. Disney would get to create the Reedy Creek Improvement District which let Disney try out new ways of handling urban issues such as waste management and other city-related issues. The Magic Kingdom itself would be built as two levels with the unseen underground much like Epcot's unseen underground of cars. Celebration, Florida, is the closes we have to Epcot, which is a real city designed by Disney.

Tron Arcade

The Tron Arcade has some ideas that sounded great such as a Laser Hologran Game, 3D Tron Adventure Game, and Electronic Playground. But these ideas were all the same as the exhibits at Epcot's ImageWorks, though it is likely it would have also had arcade games.

A few reasons the arcade never made it off the grid is the lack of initial success of the film. Also, an arcade was already in the area.

Flynn's Arcade would open in California Adventure for a short time. It would stick more closely to the movie arcade than the original Disneyland plan, but it would be open for a limited time only.

Disneyland Bowl

Disneyland Bowl would be a Downtown Disney version of the Hollywood Bowl. It was planned to be a 5000-seat amphitheater which would have been located on Harbor Blvd.

It had some opposition by locals along with other local area expansions Disney had planned.

MYST Island

MYST Island was to be located on Discovery Island. The island would have been turned into a real life version of the video game MYST. For those who are not familiar with the game, it was a non-linear game that let people explore and uncover the mysteries of the island.

Basing anything off of a popular video game can be a risk. While MYST did have sequels, it was the first one that everyone played. Besides basing an area on a game which may and did have a short bit of popularity, creating the island would have been difficult and expensive as it would require moving construction materials to and from the island with a small footprint and little room to work.

Jim Rouse Development Company Locations

Disney has started working with the Jim Rouse Development Company on a number of projects in the 1980s and 90s. These projects were similar but in different locations. None of them got completed. We already discussed one earlier which was the most ambitious: the Burbank Studio theme park.

The first would have been the Texaspostion in Dallas. This would have been a mall but a mall the Disney way. There would be a mix of retail and entertainment. There would have some rides but not full-fledged theme parks. Disney was to handle the entertainment with the Jim Rouse Development Company taking care of the retail side of things. Another location was also looked at in Chicago.

Disney and the Jim Rouse Development Company never could come up with a working location. Costs were a part of the problem. A Disney venture is not something that is cheap but is always a quality product. But that comes at a cost. A regional center does not offer enough incentive to put in the money needed as a full-fledged theme park would.

While none of the Jim Rouse Development Company ideas worked out, Disney would create similar projects on their own such as Downtown Disney on much smaller scales.

Conclusion

While you may be sad to see some great ideas that never made it, this book does have happy endings for many ideas. By now you have seen that ideas rarely go away forever at Disney. Many of these ideas may have not been built as originally planned but parts of them would make it into other projects. In some cases such as the Movie Pavilion an idea gets upgraded.

We also see that Disney is way ahead of the curve. Some of the concepts have been decades ahead of the final product. Disney often is the first in the industry in using new technology. An example is simulator technology which they had been thinking about for about a decade before finally using it. Sometimes Disney is not the first to use the technology but thinks of it long before anyone. An example is using electro-magnets for the coaster in Discovery Bay. Some of these ideas were over a decade ahead of being implemented, and some were so far ahead of their time such as the Herbie ride that they just couldn't be built.

We do see that money is often a reason that these great ideas die. However, money can't always be blamed. Other reasons out of Disney's control can kill an idea such as a lack of local support.

Disney is not just a theme park, it is an entertainment company. At times the parks can work independently of the rest of the company, with many popular rides such as Pirates and the Haunted Mansion being stand-alone rides. However the current trend demands rides that are based on popular media properties owned by Disney or that Disney can license. Original ideas that do not connect to the rest of the Disney empire like the first California Adventure Carland concept do not get made. Even ideas based on a Disney movie can fail to get made if the movie does not perform well enough. The fortunes of the rest of the Disney empire impact the park now more then ever.

It may be fun to ask what might have been but sometimes the more exciting question to ask is what will be? To paraphrase Walt, the Disney theme parks will never be completed.

About the Author

I have been a writer for over a decade, and a contributor to a local paper for a few years.

I grew up 10 minutes from Disneyland and have been a Disney fan all my life. I also have made a successful business selling Disneyana collectibles.

More Books from Theme Park Press

Theme Park Press is the largest independent publisher of Disney, Disney-related, and general interest theme park books in the world, with dozens of new releases each year.

Our authors include Disney historians like Jim Korkis and Didier Ghez, Disney animators and artists like Mel Shaw and Eric Larson, and such Disney notables as Van France, Tom Nabbe, and Bill "Sully" Sullivan, as well as many promising first-time authors.

We're always looking for new talent.

In March 2016, we published our 100th title. For a complete catalog, including book descriptions and excerpts, please visit:

ThemeParkPress.com

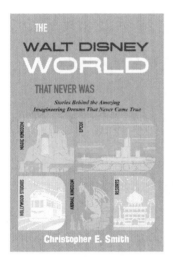

The Imagineering Graveyard

On an alternate earth, Walt Disney World guests are taking in the thrills of Thunder Mesa, braving the Beastly Kingdom, marveling at Villains Mountain, and staying the night at Disney's Persian Resort. Want to join them? This is your guidebook to the theme park that Disney never built.

themeparkpress.com/books/walt-disney-world-never-was.htm

Welcome, Foolish Readers!

Join your new Ghost Host, Jeff Baham, as he recounts the colorful, chilling history of the Haunted Mansion and pulls back the shroud on its darkest secrets in this definitive book about Disney's most ghoulish attraction. Packed with photos and never-before-told stories.

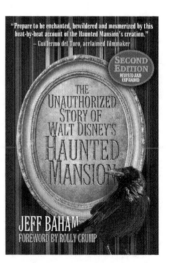

themeparkpress.com/books/haunted-mansion.htm

The Rosetta Stone of Disney Magic

Warning! There be secrets ahead. Disney secrets. Mickey doesn't want you to know how the magic is made, but Jim Korkis knows, and if you read Jim's book, you'll know, too. Put the kids to bed. Pull those curtains. Power down that iPhone. Let's keep this just between us...

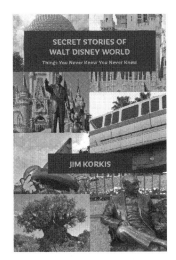

The Mouse Made EASY

Disney gurus Josh Humphrey and Dave Shute have distilled their best advice into this comprehensive, up-to-date-for-2017 book for both first-time visitors and "any-timers" who want their Disney World vacation to be both flawless and fun.

History Made Magical

Andrew Kiste pulls back the pixie dust curtain on some of the most iconic rides in the Magic Kingdom, and also pulls back the *next* curtain, revealing the historical and cultural influences that inspired Walt Disney and his Imagineers.

themeparkpress.com/books/historical-tour-disney-world-1.htm

Stuff Even Mickey Doesn't Know

When a theme park has been around for 60 years, it hides a lot of secrets. Disneyland expert Gavin Doyle has swept aside the pixie dust and uncovered little-known stories about the happiest place on earth that will make you a master of the magic.

themeparkpress.com/books/disneyland-secrets.htm

Made in the USA
Middletown, DE
15 December 2019